MW00656911

Praise for Mark Rivera and *Sideman*

"Mark Rivera has been playing saxophone with Billy Joel for more than forty years, and he somehow found time to squeeze in gigs with Ringo Starr, Simon & Garfunkel, Peter Gabriel, Hall & Oates, Foreigner, and too many others to mention. His addictive new book *Sideman* tells his entire incredible life story. It's a must-read for any serious music fan."
—Andy Greene, Senior Writer, *Rolling Stone*

"You can see why so many of rock's greatest musicians have come to rely on Mark Rivera. As his new book demonstrates time and again, the man is smart and extraordinarily empathetic, and can tell a fantastic story. An insider's look from the musician's musician, *Sideman* is a delight."
—Nathaniel Philbrick, National Book Award–winning author of *In the Heart of the Sea*

"Brooklyn, 1960's. When you grow-up there like Mark and I did, you learn there's no shortcut to hard work. You learn, you grind, you practice, you hustle. That's how you become Mark Rivera: his insane talent is a given; what makes him special is the JOY he brings—whether it's creating in the studio or rocking Madison Square Garden, artists know they're in good hands. They trust him, they love him, and the audience feels it, too. That's the secret sauce you'll find in this book: the other side of the Sideman."
—Ken Dashow, Host of Q104.3 Afternoon Drive and Sunday Morning *Breakfast with The Beatles*, iHeartMedia, New York, NY

"There isn't an instrument Mark Rivera can't play and he's traveled the world with rock 'n' roll's giants. (He even remembers what the hell happened on most of those tours!) But alongside all that talent and hustle is Mark's greatest gift: his humanity. He sounds like one of us because he is one of us. If you're ready to be inspired by the *real* people shaping the music we all love, read this book cover to cover."
—Scott Shannon, Radio Disk Jockey, New York, NY, and Host of the nationally syndicated *Scott Shannon Presents America's Greatest Hits*

"They don't make them anymore like they made Mark Rivera. He's a human jukebox—the music just comes straight away. It's equal parts innate talent and a lifetime's dedication to craft. The only thing left for him to do—because he's done everything and played with everyone—is share that experience on the page, especially with the future generations. He's that important."
—Steve Cohen, Lighting and Production Design for Billy Joel, Elton John, Daryl Hall and John Oates

"I've been working with Mark for decades. That guy you see dancing around with that smile and saxophone—it's not bullshit. He's got more energy than God. Offstage, he's as real as they come. Mark will hang with you and talk with you and bring you back up to that good place. You're gonna love these pages because when Mark gives you something, it's *always* the genuine article."

—Brian Ruggles, Front of House Sound for
Simon and Garfunkel, Billy Joel, and Foreigner

SIDEMAN

SIDEMAN
In Pursuit of the Next Gig

MARK RIVERA

with **MIKE PONCY**

Matt Holt Books
An Imprint of BenBella Books, Inc.
Dallas, TX

Matt Holt is an imprint of BenBella Books, Inc.
10440 N. Central Expressway
Suite 800
Dallas, TX 75231
benbellabooks.com
Send feedback to feedback@benbellabooks.com

BenBella and *Matt Holt* are federally registered trademarks.

Printed in the United States of America
10 9 8 7 6 5 4 3 2 1

Library of Congress Control Number: 2022031855
ISBN 9781637742990 (hardcover)
ISBN 9781637743003 (electronic)

Copyediting by James Fraleigh
Proofreading by Lisa Story and Denise Pangia
Text design and composition by PerfecType, Nashville, TN
Cover design by Brigid Pearson
Cover photo © MediaPunch Inc / Alamy Stock Photo
Printed by Lake Book Manufacturing

To Yogi Horton, Carlos Vega, T-Bone Wolk, Doug Stegmeyer,
and Bob Birch. Most especially, to Bobby Mayo.
We played together, laughed together, stuck together...
Though you are gone, I carry your songs in my heart always.

CONTENTS

PART THREE

by Ringo Starr

Sideman. I love the title because Mark, of course, is much more than that.

People sometimes think I got out of bed one day and—*poof*—I was in the Beatles. But that's not true. Before I met the lads, I was playing every damn wedding, club, and bar in Liverpool, not knowing where it was all going to go. And yeah, it went crazy for me when I met up with three of the most incredible musician-writers—brothers—in the world.

But what if all that hadn't happened? Would I still be lugging out the kit, night after night, doing what I love and putting bread on the table? Who knows, but that's what Mark has done. Even without the "big break," there he is, making music with the rest of us for the last half century.

That's quite a trick. How does he pull it off?

For the All Starr Band, I always like to have an instrumentalist—piano, guitar, congas, horns. A sideman to give a bigger picture to the sound. Anyway, I got lucky when Mark joined the band. I remember we were coming together to rehearse before going out on tour. All these headliners and then Mark, the new sideman. But in the first rehearsal, it was apparent that he not only knew every note to our songs, but he also probably knew every note to every rock song ever written. Lyrics, too. So, the sideman quickly became our musical director.

Now, I've put members of the band in charge before and it can get a bit tense—the piano player telling the guitar player what to do all the time can seriously ruin the vibe. But Mark is beautiful. Everyone loves him. He gets us all together and on the same page, and no one gets pissed. That's his gift.

Since that first rehearsal, Mark and I have become good friends. He's the kind of guy you can call anytime and know he'll be there for you. And he knows that feeling that we can't explain to anyone who doesn't play music for an audience. Some nights it's spiritual. That's the reason I do it. It's the reason Mark does it. He's not like, "Oh, it's a job." I've played with those musicians, too. Not Mark Rivera. You can never doubt Mark as a musician or as a person. His spirit is high, and I suspect it's a big reason why he's played with pretty much everyone.

But it can't have come easy. Fifty years is a long time to be doing the sideman's hustle, pulling a rabbit out of a hat every time the mortgage is due or the taxman shows up. And let's face it, rock 'n' roll isn't always good for your health.

So how does he do it? It's a good question and well worth the spotlight.

PART ONE

A kid from the old neighborhood: performing "Italian Restaurant" with one of the greatest songwriters and performers to ever grace the stage, the amazing Billy Joel. Madison Square Garden, 2022. (Credit: Myrna Suárez)

UP IN THE AIR

■ **March 2020. Delta flight 2261. Homebound from Mexico City after a Billy Joel show.**

I look out the airplane window, surveying what's beneath. A chance to get above it all. A chance to reflect. Where to begin? Looking back isn't exactly the musician's most in-tune skill:

> You did good or you fucked up. Who cares? That was four measures ago. All that matters is what's happening *now*. And if you can't get hip to that, you may as well be, I don't know—at MIT doing quantum physics or some other contemplative bullshit. Because this rhythm section is cooking, so either get with it or get off the stage.

Our craft is about staying in the present, moving forward with the music.

The flight attendant comes by with a drink. Double Ketel on the rocks, a splash of cranberry, and a lemon wedge. I say thank you. I smile. I take the time. I'm being responsive. There's a rhythm here; my job is to get hip to it.

Can't do that unless I'm keeping up with the music.

3

But then the flight attendant is gone, our micro jam session concluded. What now? I take a sip. It's true, musicians will drink to forget. But sometimes, we drink to remember—to come out of the present and, for me, be grateful. Because I've had a hell of a ride. If someone had told me when I started in this business that I'd be jumping around on stages for more than half a century, I'd have said they were fucking crazy. There are just too many hazards to even contemplate a long run like that. Burnout, suicide, overdoses, irrelevance . . .

Back in 1986, between stints with Foreigner and Billy Joel, I took a gig touring with Yoko Ono. One day after rehearsal, she brought the band up to her apartment at the Dakota. The same place she and John Lennon had lived together, the same place where John was shot and killed coming out of his limousine and entering the building. And I remember going into the apartment and seeing John's glasses on the windowsill. They were the same pair he'd been wearing the night he was murdered. One of the lenses was still caked in his blood. Yoko kept them there, she said, because it was all that she had left of him.

A decade earlier, I'd played with John at what would be his final live appearance, and now, seeing the glasses in an apartment where this man had a family and all of those things that make a life, a feeling of impermanence washed over me. John was the reason a whole generation of musicians, myself included, became rock 'n' rollers, and here was absolute proof that none of us, not even the rock immortals themselves, could predict how long we'd be around to celebrate that thing we all loved: music. And the fact that I've been blessed to make music with so many of the greats like John, night after night, year after year, is something to be thankful for. It's also something worth sharing.

I'm looking out the window again, feeling better about the prospect. I've had victories to savor, failures to mull. And it wasn't always plane rides with drinks made nice and neat. It wasn't always sold-out shows in Mexico City or Japan or Rome or wherever. Those are easy places to go—and there were some good times. But there were also a lot of rides on the B-train—gigs in shitty neighborhoods in shitty clubs with shitty drummers.

After all, none of us just appeared on the big stage. We each came from somewhere.

■ Brooklyn, New York, 1975

I borrowed the monkey suit and tie. *The collar of obedience.* My cousin, Vinny, pulled up in his 1970 Dodge Dart and honked the horn. Forty-First Street between Eighth and Ninth Avenue. The house where I grew up.

I came out the front door, shouting goodbye to my parents, and shuffled down the brick stoop with my gear and a little suitcase. The monkey suit was on a coat hanger. Vinny popped the trunk and I plopped in all my stuff: saxophone, amp, gig bag, the suitcase, and an electric bass.

Shit. If the collar of obedience wasn't enough of a reminder that I didn't want to do the gig, the bass was. We were headed to the Catskills, two hours upstate, to play Latin cocktail music for some rich folks. That was the drag—not the bass itself—but knowing that I was in for endless hours of playing nothing but *bum, bum, bum, bum* . . . all the while stuffed into some suit. Not exactly rock 'n' roll.

I unzipped the suitcase. Inside, wedged between the socks and underwear, were a couple of joints. I took out the first, closed the trunk, and hopped into the car.

I remember thinking that I needed to get as high as possible both because it was two hours to the Jewish Alps and because I was a mess. That's the way it was when you were twenty-two years old and you wanted to be a rock star—you're moving along, life feels good for a spell, like you've got it under control, and then the ground drops out from under you. Over and over again, baseless optimism followed by the inevitable fall back to earth: *You chose a musician's path, and you will therefore spend most of your time just trying to get on your feet and figuring out what the hell you're doing.*

So, what was I doing? I'd been in more bands than I had hairs on my head: Home Brew, Our Gang, General Meek, Essence . . . and those were only the ones we'd bothered to name. I was always picking up other gigs: *Hey Mark, I got this thing out in Queens. Bring your guitar . . . Hey Mark, you sing great! Wanna come out to the East Village tonight? . . . Hey Mark, grab your sax and let's head up to the Upper East Side and sit in with those cats . . .* I was all over the city, five, six, seven nights a week. I was hustling. Or at least telling myself I was. Because the hustle is about real bread, and I wasn't making any.

Vinny steered us out of the city, and I tried to stay upbeat. It had been a while since we'd hung out and I didn't want to be a drip to my big cousin, who was more of an older brother to me. We grew up two blocks apart and my mother was always leery of him because we'd usually get into some kind of trouble. Mostly because I was always wanting to impress Vinny. He'd say, "You know, you should be a stuntman," and he'd have me rolling down the stairs or falling off a garage roof.

Then he'd say, "Yeah, that was good, you should do it again."

And I'd be like, "Okay, Vinny."

But our real bond was always music. Listening to it, playing out—neither of us could get enough, and we'd been in and out of bands together throughout junior high and high school.

So here I was again, tagging along with Vinny to his weekend gig. He knew I needed the dough. Their bass player had just quit, and Vinny talked the band leader into giving me the spot—*My cousin can play anything you fuckin' got on any fuckin' instrument you want.*

Vinny was always talking me up like that.

It was at a place called the Raleigh Hotel up in the Catskills. The deal was two hundred dollars for two shows, Friday and Saturday night. Vinny said we'd be driving back to Brooklyn right after the second show, when I anticipated we'd be stoned out of our minds. (Not like I could afford it. But, like I said, you needed the grass to make it through the doldrums.)

The windows were rolled down and the sticky summer air was finally moving. "You *can* play these bass parts, right?" Vinny asked. I told him it was no problem. He kept talking, warning me that the band leader was kind of an asshole and not to let him get under my skin, and about the set list and the chord changes. I was nodding, only half-listening because the pot was doing its thing and the trees were going by, lush and green. I wasn't worried about the chord changes. I simply didn't want to do the gig or meet the stupid band leader or deal with any of this shit. I was twenty-two years old, back living with my parents, making no money, and the idea of the rock 'n' roll dream was getting further and further away. The only thing getting closer was the rotten gig, and I really wanted Vinny to just stop yapping and keep driving, past the hotel so we could get up into the mountains and, I don't know, become Buddhist monks or something.

How did it get this way? Ever since I was a kid, I'd dreamed of becoming a rock star, not some guy schlepping upstate to play cocktail gigs. What the hell happened to the dream?

2

COUNTING STEPS

■ Brewster, New York, 2020

We got back from Mexico City, and then they canceled Billy's next show at Madison Square Garden. There's a virus. It was on the news starting a few months ago. It's been coming, like a wave, and now everyone has to stay put for a bit. But I'm not good at staying put—I've been gigging since I was thirteen.

So, I'm home—the same house my wife, Sandra, and I bought back in 1984 when I was between gigs (Billy's An Innocent Man and Foreigner's Agent Provocateur tours)—and I'm sitting in my favorite room in the house. Windows all around. Another perch to gaze and reflect. I'm thinking about how important music is to me. Ever since I was a kid, music just resonated with something inside. Because you can't teach someone to sing in tune and you can't teach someone to dance in time. You either have good pitch or good rhythm, or you don't. It speaks to you innately and turns that something on.

Miles Davis said that if you play one note right, everything else just makes sense. He was referring to tone, the quality of the sound: its pitch, its shape. What were those initial tones for me? When did music start making sense?

I gaze out the windows. The light is dim beneath the gray sky. We can't play music right now. But there are buds on the trees, and a whole world is ready to emerge.

■ Brooklyn, 1959-1961

When I was six or seven years old, I used to blink my eyes a lot. My mother would freak out. "He needs to be tested," she'd tell my father.

But my father was a very patient man. "Angie, don't worry about it, it'll pass," he'd say. And he was right.

But I had a lot of quirks.

Like, when I walked around the house or the neighborhood with my pals, I would purposely drag my left big toe along the ground. Just a little bit. So instead of the even:

left, right, left, right, left, right . . .

it was:

DRAG, step, DRAG, step, DRAG, step . . .

For some reason, I felt that my left foot wasn't getting as much attention as my right foot, and I was off kilter, like a gymnast about to fall off the balance beam. So, I would compensate, consciously dragging that toe along the ground to keep me steady—to keep me on the balance beam. Of course, every month or so, my left sneaker would have a huge hole in it, and I'd need a new pair. That would drive my mother *crazy*.

I couldn't help it—I was compelled to always be making things even. Like if I scratched my left ear, at some point, even if it was like two minutes later, I needed to balance the ledger and scratch my right ear.

Also, I was *obsessed* with numbers, particularly the number 5. I would tap, say, the kitchen counter, with my right hand *five* times. But that wasn't enough because I could also tap it with each of my *five* digits *five* times:

[thumb] *1, 2, 3, 4, 5* . . . [index] *1, 2, 3, 4, 5* . . .
[middle] *1, 2, 3, 4, 5.* . . . [ring] *1, 2, 3, 4, 5* . . . [pinky] *1, 2, 3, 4, 5.*

And of course, if I did it with my right hand, I had to follow with my left:

[left thumb] 1, 2, 3, 4, 5 . . . [left index] 1, 2, 3, 4, 5 . . . [left middle] 1, 2, 3, 4, 5 . . . [left ring] 1, 2, 3, 4, 5 . . . [left pinky] 1, 2, 3, 4, 5.

I'd tap my face, my neck, my shoulder, the doorknobs, the door jamb, the floor, the stereo, the cabinet . . . whatever. Tedious to some but soothing to me. Why? I have no idea except to say it felt good, like it was providing a consistency to my day. It was comforting to know there was something to fill up each moment and keep me from drifting. I guess it made me feel grounded. Like the more I touched things, the more I understood they were there and so was I.

But what if I stopped doing any of these things? Would that somehow *unbalance* my little kid universe and send things flying into outer space? I hoped not. So, I didn't dare give any of them up. I had faith in these quirks, and I practiced them religiously. And the ritual that I practiced with the utmost dedication was *counting steps* as I went up and down stairways.

For example, there were five steps that led up to our house from the street where my friends and I played stoopball:

1, 2, 3, 4, 5 . . .

And then there was a sixth step that would go into the hallway:

6 . . .

Our house was multi-family and my grandparents lived in the two-bedroom upstairs just above us. My grandmother was cooking all the time and the entryway would always smell like good food. So, if I came in from my stoopball and smelled cookies, I would then run up *those* stairs and the count would continue:

7, 8, 9, 10, 11, 12, 13, 14, 15, 16, 17, 18, 19, 20 . . .

Or if she and my grandfather were making tomato sauce in the basement, I would go down instead of up and it would now be a subtraction problem:

5, 4, 3, 2, 1, 0, –1, –2, –3, –4, –5 . . .

The combinations were endless because, like any kid, I never stayed in the same place for very long. Why would I? I loved my house, my family, my friends, my neighborhood. *Plenty of steps!* So, I was up and down all the time, keeping my counts and whatever new permutations I'd formulated as I went about my day.

And counting stairs *was* a habit my mother endorsed. The blinking was gone, and it was obvious that her son, while a little different, was a happy, social, and full-of-energy kid.

He also seemed to be good at numbers and math.

■ ■ ■

When I was probably about eight, my father had a Spanish guitar he would just kind of strum. He didn't know what he was doing but I loved the sound. We'd be in the living room, and he would smile, and I would put my finger on the fretboard, and I'd know that if I wanted the sound to get higher, I would go this way; lower, go that way. I was simply reacting.

The front steps leading to the family apartments in
Brooklyn, circa 1960. (Credit: Rivera Family Collection)

There's something that happens when you make an instrument work. It begins with that very first note you learn to play. It touches something in you. I don't know how, why, or what, but you're inspired by it. So, you keep going.

You start being musical.

I remember I would watch *The Three Stooges*, and they had a couple of songs that I'd sing perfectly. And my Uncle Vinny—another Vinny—said, "You know, he's got really good pitch. I'll give him a couple lessons on the saxophone."

So, my uncle taught me, and I'd be watching the way his fingers worked. It was a variation on my "fives" ritual, only the sequences were more interesting and meaningful: when done in a particular order, they produced a particular melody line. Once my uncle showed me how the combinations went, suddenly one of my compulsions was now producing these tones, which filled my ears and my whole body.

So Mom and Dad bought me a saxophone, which Uncle Vinny sourced when it probably fell off the back of a truck. And within a few months I was better than my uncle, so my parents sent me to Professor Cavolo once every week for three dollars. My father would come with me, and I made sure to practice because I was terrified that I would let my father down for $3, which was a lot of money back then. But I had trouble reading the notes. They just kind of ran all over the page—a big, jumbled mess. So, I'd listen to what Professor Cavolo would play and I'd go home, and I'd remember how the phrasing went and practice.

Then I'd pick up my dad's guitar and play the notes there. It was like counting steps:

Dots and spaces, 5, 7, 9, 11—all the spaces on the fretboard.

I had my own patterns on both instruments and, using these patterns, I would play the piece of music correctly.

Only when Professor Cavolo would point to a particular line on the music sheet would I totally fuck it up because, again, the notes on the page were a giant mess. But the professor kept me on board. He knew I had an ear and a system to memorize what I heard. And three bucks a week was three bucks a week.

So I played and played. I enjoyed it so much, I just did it. I mean, the hardest thing to do on the saxophone is get a good sound, and you play long tones during lessons and practice. It's boring as shit. But that's what makes it happen. And within a few months, I had these calluses on my fingers that meant I could play for hours. I didn't feel it. Through all the spurts and flubs, the instrument was speaking to me, making sense of things.

And I wanted it to say more.

3

SHINING OVER BROOKLYN

Brewster, New York, 2020

Sandra and I are quarantined because we both caught the virus. We'd cut down our movements, acted responsibly, but it still happened. Sandra went over to help a woman at her house, and the woman called a few days later and said, "I don't feel well."

Sandra had worn a mask, but within seventy-two hours, we both had fevers.

But now we're on the backside of it and Sandra has returned to staying busy. Winter is over, she says, and it's time to plant a garden. So we spent the weekend outside, working in the dirt.

My wife amazes me. Born and raised just outside of Zurich, she is the ultimate Swiss Miss. If you're on time, you're late. This is how things are. I'd come home from the road, being away four, six weeks sometimes, and I'd say, "Let's keep the kids home from school tomorrow," and Sandra would say, "No." And I'd say, "Well, how about we—"

"No," she'd interrupt, "if you change the rules to fit your situation, then they're not really rules. And if you don't adhere to that, then it winds up being like, 'Oh, whatever the hell happens, happens.'"

So, we're quarantined at the house, and we have more than we need. I turn on the water, and there's water. I open the refrigerator and there's food. These are all things where you have to say, "By God's grace I still have plenty." So, as we planted our garden together–tilling soil, sowing seeds, watering them in–I tried to let that feeling of gratitude wash over me. Because I, too, sprouted from a simple place under the sun. I, too, am the sum of every good, bad, and indifferent action, relationship, conversation, whatever . . .

Everything that's ever happened in my life, I am the end product of it.

■ Over Brooklyn, Saturday morning, circa 1965

Beneath, spread out as far as the eye can see, are the apartments and houses of thousands of multigenerational families, each waking to a new day in their quest to make it in a New World. Out of some of these homes, scattered around, middle-school-aged children begin to appear, like ants out of a great mound's many tunnels. Clutched in their hands are instruments of some kind—a horn, a drum, a violin. Music has been speaking to them and, rain or shine, they answer the call.

■ ■ ■

I was one of those kids. My father would load me and my saxophone into the car and drive the twenty minutes to Empire Boulevard and New York Avenue for Brooklyn Borough-Wide Band practice. It was offered to a select group of middle school musicians who showed talent and dedication to their instrument. And every Saturday, for two hours, my father would sit in the rehearsal hall, a content smile on his face, and listen to a stage full of thirteen- and fourteen-year-olds make noise. He would never miss it.

My father worked as a teletype operator for RCA Communications. He typed amazingly well. I don't know how he learned to type like that. It was before fax machines and before RCA became automated. What he would type went into pneumatic tubes that shot the communiqué this way and that for overseas transmission. Years later, when they finally automated, he ran RCA's computers.

He worked three different shifts. There was four to midnight: he'd get home around 12:30, sleep through the night, wake up, and spend the afternoons with us. Then there was 6 AM to 2 PM, his favorite shift because he'd leave the house at 5:30 AM, go to work at 6, and come home by 2:30. So, even if I was at school, I'd be coming home in time for us to have the whole day together. And then there was midnight to 8 AM, the graveyard shift. He'd get home about 8:30 AM, sleep a few hours, and start the day again. No matter what the shift, he *never* complained. Sometimes the guy worked double shifts, and I never knew anybody happier to do it for his family than my father.

And he provided. We didn't have a lot, but we never thought we didn't have enough. I remember my parents used to get me these jeans—I was skinny as a rail, they'd get me like a size 22 or 24 waist, and they'd get the length like really, really long. So, being a kid, I'd skin my knees, and my mother would put a patch on the knee, and six months later, the patch would be up by my thigh. I hadn't outgrown the waist, but I was taller, and you'd see all of these patches crawling up my thigh instead of over the knee I'd scraped.

My father's childhood hadn't been fortunate. He came to the Harlem projects straight from Puerto Rico when he was twelve. He spoke no English and was told by his father he needed to get a job to help support the family. Somehow, he'd made it all work—he learned the language, excelled in the local public schools, and put food on the table. He didn't talk about it much, and it wasn't until I was older that I really understood the perseverance of this man, but you just got the sense that Dad was always a happy camper. A contented soul whose glass was always halfway full. And that gratitude was infectious. I can remember as a kid coming into the house and seeing my parents dancing or holding hands. They were very much in love, and Mom, who would stutter whenever she got nervous, always looked so relaxed and content when my father was nearby. She, like the rest of us, loved to be around him.

Dad and me in 1984, celebrating Foreigner's album 4 and my success with the band. A hard worker and the consummate family man, Dad immigrated to America as a kid without knowing a lick of English or a dime in his pocket. (Credit: Rivera Family Collection)

There's an expression he had—*come sin vergüenza*, which means "eat without shame." In other words, if you're eating a peach, take the bite and let the juice run down your chin—don't let your pleasure embarrass you. My father believed a person should always live like that: dance like no one is looking, sing like no one is listening. Just enjoy it and be totally absorbed in the moment.

And my father adored music. Jazz. Classical. Latin. We had this great stereo system (like my saxophone, it fell off the truck and Uncle Vinny was there to scoop it up), and my father would record his favorite weekly program on WRVR, Riverside Radio. It was jazz with a DJ named Ed Beach who would do an hour-long set of a particular artist—A Night with Charlie Parker, A Night with Lester Young, A Night with Dizzy Gillespie, A Night with Coleman Hawkins—and my father would run the tape very slowly so it would last for the whole program. Then during the week, he'd sit down and listen to the music, and you could see him get totally absorbed in the sound.

It wasn't just jazz programs; it was the Latin music, too, and my father would dance around the living room and be unabashedly swept away by the music. Or a piece of classical music would come on and he would close his eyes, rock his head, and the music would take him away. And if it happened to be a piece of music he could sing along to, he'd sing like it didn't matter what anybody else thought. I remember being a little boy and looking at him, seeing his joy, and it would make me happy without my even knowing why. He was willing to share these moments with me, show me that it was okay to be overcome with something beautiful and take it all in.

So, when I would go to my room and take the saxophone out of my hope chest and play it in the entryway to our building, where the acoustics of the stairwell and hall would allow the sound to reverberate and swell and bounce around me, I too would permit myself to be overcome, to let the joy wash over me. My father was not a musician, but he, more than anyone, showed me that the best way to play music was to *celebrate* music.

■ ■ ■

"He should see a live performance," my father told my mother. I was only ten years old, but my father knew I had the bug. He saw the way I'd gravitate toward the living room when he'd turn on the stereo. He heard me relentlessly playing those long tones in the hall, saw the calluses on my fingers; he understood I was getting better.

So, Dad bought two tickets to Harlem's Apollo Theatre to see the legendary saxophonist Sonny Rollins. I, of course, knew who Rollins was because my father's radio shows would talk about him and Dad had all his records, including his new album, *Golden Disk*. This record was enthralling because Rollins, a bit of an eccentric, was pictured on the album cover with this huge goatee and a mohawk haircut. I'd stare at that wild man's picture while my dad spun his record, telling me how Rollins, who had also grown up in Harlem, had previously quit touring and would go out to the Williamsburg Bridge every day for like fourteen or fifteen hours straight, playing his saxophone, trying to perfect his sound, while people who probably didn't know they'd just passed one of the world's best musicians thought, *Hey, that guy's pretty good.*[1] Now my father was taking me to see him play and I was over the moon.

We took the subway into Manhattan, up to 125th Street, and walked the few blocks to the Apollo. Other than visiting family, we didn't venture out of Brooklyn too often, and certainly not for concerts, so this was a big deal. I remember walking into the theater and my father telling me that lots of famous people played here,

---

1. Rollins's sabbatical up on the Williamsburg Bridge lasted three years and resulted in his groundbreaking 1962 album, *The Bridge*.

including James Brown and the Famous Flames, whose recent album *Live at the Apollo* was at #2 on the pop record chart.[2]

The night's opening act was the Jimmy Smith Trio. Smith, who was this skinny Black guy, came out on the stage very humbly, almost apologetically, and sat down at his organ and began turning knobs. Though we were up in the balcony, I could see the sweat beading on his face beneath the spotlights. He kept wiping his brow with the sleeve of his suit, and I suddenly felt very nervous for him, like maybe he wasn't going to play well because he seemed so shy and because of the sweat running down his face. But then his hands started pressing the organ keys and there was this rich, gospel tone suddenly wobbling around, filling up the entire theater like a bathtub fills with water. And the audience, which was primarily African American, applauded as Smith, his fingers now dancing along the keys and turning more dials, literally spoke to the organ, having a conversation with it while the guitar player and drummer just sat back, not playing a single note yet, and let Smith continue to open things up. Then the trio was in full swing, the snare and the ride cymbal and the electric guitar in sync with the organ, and the crowd applauded and praised the man behind the organ, who was now completely given over to the sound. It was intoxicating.

Smith's forty-minute set was followed by a short film, a documentary or something; I don't have any idea what that was about.

---

2. Interestingly, Brown himself footed the bill for the recording of *Live at the Apollo*, as his label and management didn't think new recordings of previously released material would sell. Brown disagreed and demanded they be released, and now the record sits in the Grammy Hall of Fame and was ranked #65 in *Rolling Stone* magazine's 2020 update of their 500 Greatest Albums of All Time. James Brown was right, the execs were wrong. Go figure . . . (https://www.rollingstone.com/music/music-lists/best-albums-of-all-time-1062063/the-band-music-from-big-pink-2-1063133/)

And then Sonny Rollins came out. This guy on the album cover—*that one with the mohawk*—only now the sounds were being created up on stage, right in front of me beneath the long white-hot spotlights. And his fingers were moving and his lips puffing, working to achieve the sounds, and there was no fear in his playing, only the willingness to be in the moment and allow the emotions to wash over him.

I'd never experienced anything like it. Sure, I'd heard the records—Sonny Rollins, Lester Young, Dexter Gordon, all these great cats—but to witness this guy on stage and the crowd's reaction was something entirely different. More than anything, I was blown away by the way Rollins commanded the instrument. I'd only been playing saxophone for a couple of years, but something inside was telling me that I wanted to be like this man—to stand on a stage, surrounded by great players and in front of an amazing audience, and just put it out there. *Come sin vergüenza.*

SWITCHING TO COLOR

4

■ Growing up, we never had a color TV until I don't know what year. Before that, everyone made this big deal about *Walt Disney's Wonderful World of Color* on NBC, the first color TV show. I was about nine or ten years old and Tinkerbell would touch the peacock with her wand, and it would turn from black and white to color, but we'd watch it on our black-and-white TV, so I'd say, "I don't see what's the big freaking deal," because, of course, it didn't do anything. Then one evening, I was at a neighbor's house, and they did have a color TV. Sure enough, when Tinkerbell struck the peacock, I was like, "Whoa! *That's* what they're talking about!"

■ **February 9, 1964 (eleven years old)**
It started out like any other Sunday afternoon.

Mom and Dad would load us into the car, and we'd head up to Ninety-Ninth and Park Avenue to visit my dad's parents and sister. They lived in the projects, which was always a little jarring—all these people squeezed into floor after floor of tiny railroad apartments. I remember there were incinerators on every level for

23

people's garbage. On the way up to my grandparents' unit, the elevator would stop at the different floors, the door would open, and the smell of burnt garbage would drift in from the hallway, mixed with whatever ethnic foods happened to be on the stove in nearby apartments. So the third floor might smell like Cuban rice and beans and burnt garbage, the ninth floor like liver and onions and burnt garbage. Even for a kid from Brooklyn, it was stifling.

My grandparents lived on the eleventh floor (my grand-mother's Puerto Rican food and burnt garbage). My father would knock on the door, and his sister, Iris, would answer. *Titi* Iris was a spinster—she lived with her parents in the projects her entire life. She was also my godmother, and I don't know if she took extra pride in the role because she didn't have a family of her own, but she'd spoil me and my sisters—at first just my older sister, then both when my younger sis arrived—a little bit on these visits. There would always be something for us, like a small toy or a pack of baseball cards with a stick of gum.

Titi would let us into the apartment, leaving the incinerator stench in the hallway, and my grandmother, *Abuela*, would come out of the kitchen to give us kisses. Lots of them. She moved slowly because she was very diabetic and her eyesight was bad, but she would laugh and exclaim things that I only sort of understood.

Abuela's world basically ended at the front door. Titi Iris did the shopping, and my grandfather would always be going out throughout the week and coming back with guests who'd stay for dinner, so she was essentially chained to the kitchen. But, like my father, she was a joyous person. She'd always have two or three little parrots or parakeets in a cage in the living room, and there must have been fifty plants throughout the house. She'd close all the windows and let the birds out and they'd be flying around while she'd water the bright green plants, singing in Spanish to them and to the birds in her beautiful voice. Eventually, my grandfather,

Abuelo, would get up from his rocking chair, all pissed off, and he'd huff and puff "Juanita!" and tell her to shut the damn cage. And she'd just chuckle and say okay and eventually put the birds back.

I never remember Abuelo coming to answer the door. *Ever.* He was always in the living room, sitting stoically on the couch or in the rocking chair, and we'd have to march in and give him a hug and kiss. Thirty years earlier, he'd arrived in the US with his young family and gotten a shift at the Hershey's chocolate factory. A year into the job, while he was chopping blocks of chocolate, something took off one of his hands, and the factory said, "Okay, I guess we need to find someone else." He had never really been able to work since. And now he was an old man, lording over this tiny apartment, his right wrist wrapped in a leather pouch tucked close to his chest.

For me, my grandparents' bedroom was the most fascinating room in the house, and the one place I wasn't supposed to go. But tell a kid, "Don't do that," and what's the first thing he does? So, at some point during each visit, when everyone was eating or watching TV, I'd sneak into the bedroom. I remember the smell of incense and this very deep, dark painting of the Virgin Mary holding her baby, and beneath the picture was a cross and a tiny altar with pictures of all the different saints and lighted candles. A *bunch* of candles. It was Abuela's little church and sometimes, if we arrived before noon, she would still be in the bedroom, listening to the Sunday Mass broadcast on the Spanish radio station, and you would hear her reciting the words and singing the hymns. Across from the altar, next to the bed, was a large dresser, and one time I'd found a switchblade in one of Abuelo's drawers. I'd listen for anyone coming out of the kitchen, then I'd take out the switchblade and fiddle with the latch and open and close the knife. Abuelo never caught me in the room, but Titi Iris busted me a few times. She'd just say, "Mark, you know you don't belong in here," and take me out to join the others.

25

■ ■ ■

It was probably about two o'clock in the afternoon on this particular Sunday when Titi Iris surprised my sister and me with a trip to Korvette's. The three of us left the projects and walked the ten or so blocks to the discount department store, and I don't remember what my sister got, but Titi took me to the record department, and I remember wondering what I was going to pick out. I really didn't have any of my own records at that point.

But Titi said, "I'm getting you this," handing me a record with four guys on the cover. I'd heard one of the songs listed on the jacket, "I Wanna Hold Your Hand," a few times on the radio with my friends and I thought it was okay. But Titi was adamant, and it wasn't like I was gonna say, "No thanks." So we headed back to the projects, record in hand. (I'm sure Titi also got us some trinkets, like blowing bubbles or a bouncy ball.)

I can still remember sitting on the living room floor when Titi put the album on. My grandparents had one of those consoles with a TV, radio, and a record player. The first thing I heard was John Lennon singing the line, "It won't be long, yeah," and I freaked out. By the time the song was over, I knew it was the coolest thing I'd ever heard, and those very dramatic, half-shadowed faces on the front cover of *Meet the Beatles!* were suddenly mystery men who I wanted to get to know.

And with each song, the music just got better and better. Now I was staring at the back side of the album with the inset photo of the four hanging out in their boots. They looked like real friends, like a real band, and made it seem like making music together was fun. They had an attitude, and I was digging it.

But I still didn't know what was about to happen that night—that these guys were going to be on *The Ed Sullivan Show*—until Titi told me after we'd listened through the album. It was the reason she'd bought it for me, she said. So we ate dinner and dessert, the latter probably a three-layered concoction of Jell-O and pudding that Titi would make. (It would be three different colors—like green Jell-O on the bottom, tapioca or butterscotch pudding in the middle, and cherry Jell-O on top—and we'd say, "Wow!" like kids in a candy store or at the soda fountain.) And then we were all gathered in front of the TV, three generations of us in that tiny apartment:

Ladies and gentlemen, the Beatles.

And there they were, mystery men no longer.

Wow, I thought, back on the floor next to my grandmother's caged birds, my eyes glued to the TV screen. The confidence, the joy, the cohesiveness, the girls going wild . . . *I want to be just like these guys.*

Hook, line, and sinker . . . Brooklyn, 1964.
(Credit: Rivera Family Collection)

5

A BUNCH OF WHITE KIDS FROM BROOKLYN

A few years ago, a friend of mine, one of Billy's drivers who didn't grow up in the city, asked me, "So, what was it like when you were a kid in Brooklyn? Were there a lot of fights?"

I said, "Yeah, people fought all the time."

He goes, "Did you get into a lot of fights? Were you hurt often?"

I told him, "I've never been in a fight in my life."

And the guy looked in the rearview mirror and said, "You've never had a single fight?"

"Nope."

I could tell he didn't believe me. He's a friend of mine—he knows I'm not a hothead—but people hear "Brooklyn" and they assume, "Oh, you must have been scrappin' a lot as a kid."

But I wasn't. I got punched once, on the chin when I was twelve, but it was over before it started. I can't even remember the kid's name. We were playing dodgeball and I thought he was already out, and he threw the ball and pegged me. So I pushed him, and the kid turned around and fucking clocked me. He then said, "In the schoolyard, three o'clock."

And I was thinking, *Oh, shit. What should I do?* Because now I was in real trouble.

Fortunately, the kid's friends told him, "Hey, Mark's cool. He's a musician." The kid looked at me and said, "Listen, you pushed me. And it wasn't right." I apologized, and he goes, "We're good."

That was it, my one altercation. Certainly not a fight, at least by that neighborhood's standards.

So how did I grow up around all these hitters without needing to ever throw a punch? A big part of it was my dad's influence—the love and patience he demonstrated toward finding peaceful solutions in our household seemed to rub off on me. But in a tough neighborhood, that only gets you so far. Sooner or later, you find yourself pushing a kid and being told, "Three o'clock, behind the school."

The other part was music. After the Beatles were on *Ed Sullivan*, it seemed there was a new band on the show each week for the next three years—the Animals, Herman's Hermits, the Rolling Stones, the Doors. And the more I saw, the more I understood I wanted to be up on stage in a rock 'n' roll band. So, I didn't go looking for fights and fights didn't come looking for me—the other kids just sort of respected who I was: a rocker.

■ Brooklyn, New York, 1966

My cousin Vinny lived on Eighth Avenue between Forty-First and Forty-Second. There was a Chinese laundry on the ground floor, and we practiced in the basement. Like me, the neighborhood kids saw on *The Ed Sullivan Show* how cool those guys were—and how the girls went wild. So we set the drums up and managed to put a little PA system together. We even eventually had a name—Population 4—which we thought was super clever because, you know, there were four guys in the band: Cousin Vinny on lead guitar; Daryl Leoce on drums; Joel Leoce on rhythm guitar; and me on bass, vocals, and sax.

The problem was that only one of us knew how to really play instruments. So, I had to teach everybody the parts. I remember, for the song "Secret Agent Man,"[1] the other kids would lose their minds trying to learn the notes and chords, and I'd be like, "It's so freaking easy." And they'd hear me play it on my guitar or horn, and I'd show them how the parts worked, but then they'd screw it up. No one knew what the hell they were doing.

But being cool is a great motivator, and guys would actually take their instruments home and practice. It's funny, but what every music teacher in America perpetually struggles with—getting kids to practice—was something rock 'n' rollers accomplished every time they took the stage. And it wasn't just the Saturday morning band geeks who wanted to rock out; it was the slackers, too. They wanted to be like the guys on TV, like the guys on the radio. So they picked up an instrument and threw themselves at it, and pretty soon bands like Population 4 knew a few tunes.

The first gig we ever played was a Brooklyn bowling alley, Melody Lanes in Sunset Park. I was thirteen years old, in the seventh grade. Someone's father had a big Buick, and we loaded up our gear: a set of drums and a couple of amplifiers and guitars. It all fit with the trunk open, and we made our way to the gig, which was only four blocks away.

There we asked the manager where we should set up. He threw a couple of people off their lanes and told us to set up on the machine behind the belt where the balls come out. So we were

---

1. Every kid in America knew this song from the hit TV show, *Secret Agent*. Performed by Jonny Rivers, it peaked at #3 on the *Billboard* Hot 100.

actually on the lanes, careful not to drag our wires through the neighboring lanes because balls and pins were flying everywhere.

I remember looking out over the crowd, which was like ten people because everyone else in the place was bowling. My parents were there, and my dad was smiling, giving me a thumbs-up. He'd bought me boots for the gig. I wanted Beatles boots, but he said they weren't good for my feet, so he got these brown boots with no heel at all and a round toe instead of the pointers. They were lame, but at least I had boots. My bass guitar was strapped around my neck and my saxophone was nearby for when I needed it. I looked over at Daryl to see if he was ready and he was grinning ear to ear. "I can't believe I'm a drummer in a band!" he shouted, and we both laughed and then I looked at our two guitarists. Vinny was twenty yards away for some reason—probably because we couldn't find a second power outlet any closer—so he might as well have been in Cleveland, but he and Joel gave me nods, their expressions somewhere between delight and sheer terror.

Four kids from Brooklyn, about to rock.

Daryl counted us in, and we started the set, our volume barely audible over the bowling balls crashing against the pins. But then the manager came running out, waving his arms, yelling, "Stop! Stop! Stop!" I thought he was going to tell us we were too loud, but he said we couldn't start until after the national anthem. So, after a few minutes, they played "The Star-Spangled Banner" over the PA system and then we (and the bowlers) got things started again.

We had exactly three songs: "Secret Agent Man," "Steppin' Stone,"[2] and "Kicks."[3] Simple tunes. We got through the set,

---

2. Performed by the Monkees, "(I'm Not Your) Steppin' Stone" was the first B-side to chart for the band, rising to #20 in the US in 1966.

3. *Rolling Stone* magazine ranked "Kicks" as #400 on their 500 Greatest Songs of All Time. It was written for the Animals but lead singer Eric Burdon

which was supposed to be like twelve minutes but only ran eight. So, we scrambled and played "Secret Agent Man" again. Imagine that. A four-song set weighing in at twelve minutes total, and one of the songs we played *twice*.

We wrapped and said thank you, and I'm not sure anyone gave a crap. They were too busy celebrating a good roll or bemoaning gutter balls. But we were ecstatic. We'd just played our first gig.

Other kids in the neighborhood heard about the band and we ended up doing a few parties. I think we used to get like $10 to play a party, so $2.50 apiece. One time, we played a job, and the guy said, "I'm going to pay you $10 for the gig," then asked, "You guys want pizza?" *Oh yeah.* So he got us two pizzas and soda, and at the end of the night, he gave us like $6. *What the fuck?* He charged us for the two pizzas. And we got, basically, nothing. We played for pizza. So, there was a learning curve.

Population 4 lasted two more months. Then we got this guy, Fat Jerry, whose real name was Jerry D'Angelo. He was Vinny's cousin, which made him my second cousin. Fat Jerry was seventeen years old and got us into Black rhythm and blues and soul music. He said people his age wanted to hear that music while they danced and made out with each other. So we changed our name to Maitrex Square because Fat Jerry said, "It sounds British," and started to learn the tunes.

We were following the lead of the Beatles, enjoying our own revolution and exploring different influences, particularly rhythm and blues songwriting and playing styles. Everything from Smokey Robinson, the Four Tops, and of course, Motown artists, to the more up-and-coming acts like George Clinton and his band,

---

declined to record it. Instead, Paul Revere & The Raiders released it as a single, rising to #1 in Canada and #4 in the States. Sorry, Eric.

Parliament.[4] Taking all of that on eventually gave us confidence. It meant we could be a bunch of white kids from Brooklyn and play and sing this stuff, too.

---

4. If you're unfamiliar with the out-of-this-world funkiness of Parliament, do yourself a favor and give a listen to "Give Up the Funk (Tear the Roof off the Sucker)." As a single, it sold more than a million copies and put this band on the map forever.

6

OPEN WIDE

Brewster, New York, 2020

I called an old friend up yesterday. We were in a couple bands together in high school. We're just chatting, and I asked, "How is everything going?" He tells me he's got liver cancer and I'm like, "Whoa." And then he tells me that another friend of ours from the neighborhood has early-onset dementia. Then he tells me yet another friend of ours passed away.

I was only calling him up to ask him how things are going, and he says, "Yeah man, I have the liver cancer, I'm a year into my chemo." It's tough to hear a guy who's sixty-six years old—he'll be sixty-seven a month from now—dealing with liver cancer for the past year. I mean, all I ever worry about is if my blood pressure goes up when I get aggravated or whatever.

I hate hearing about friends not doing well. It just brings up so much. Because we were all young once, and we all had dreams and paths we were taking to achieve those dreams.

■ Brooklyn, 1967-1969

I don't know how my grandmother put up with me—the fucking music was so loud, and it'd go on for hours and hours. I'd lie there between the speakers and crank it.

My father had these electrostatic speakers. I don't know how he got them; most likely they, too, fell off a truck, and my Uncle Vinny scooped them up. But they were the best speakers I'd ever heard, certainly the best in the neighborhood. And it was a small apartment—the living room was probably twelve feet wide—and I'd turn the speakers inward, so they were pointing right at me lying on the floor. I'd be buried in the sound, the stereo image crystal clear, and I'd hear stuff—say, Jeff Beck on second guitar in the mix—that nobody heard because they were stuck hearing the mono version of it. Same thing with Hendrix—I could tell you when Hendrix coughed, I was so close to these records.

Nineteen sixty-seven was the most fertile year in rock 'n' roll history. Hendrix put out *Are You Experienced* and *Axis: Bold as Love*, the Beatles put out *Magical Mystery Tour* and *Sgt. Pepper's Lonely Hearts Club Band*, and Cream put out *Disraeli Gears* and *Fresh Cream*. A record would come out and you'd want to hear it, and then you couldn't wait for someone to release the next one. Back then, bands were pushing their creative limits all the time. Want to get inspired? Shit, in 1967 all you had to do was head down to the record store.

My ears were opening up. I was receiving the education that would eventually take me all over the world. Maybe Grandma sensed that. She and my mother never told me to turn the music off, which was pretty amazing because, really, it was very loud. My mother might go upstairs to my grandmother's apartment and watch TV, but I can't imagine they and the rest of the neighbors didn't hear the music. But everyone must have sensed that it was doing something to the kid in apartment A, and that all of this music was bringing about a conscious choice: rock 'n' roll was what he wanted to do with his life.

■ ■ ■

So, by the time I got into the High School of Performing Arts in NYC, my ears were wide open. I had already spent two years in the borough-wide bands that my father took me to every Saturday morning.

The high school was amazing. These were kids from every different junior high school. They took the best of the kids that played really well and placed them into symphonic bands and orchestras, so you had to have your shit together.

Population 4's first gig: (left to right) Joel, me, Daryl, and Vinny. Check out those outfits! No doubt we purchased them at The Leading Male, a men's fashion store on Kings Highway in Brooklyn. 1966. (Credit: The Leoce Family)

There were four music classes in the morning and four academic subjects in the afternoon. The first class was Piano. You sat in a room with eight different kids, and everyone learned the fingering of a piano scale. The second class would've been Ear Training, where the teacher would play a four-part piece and you had to write down what the bass note was, where the top melodies were going, and then the inner voices. The most important class of all was Theory—you learned about what each chord meant. Previously, I'd play something simple like a 1-4-5 blues progression, and I had no idea what that meant until I was in high school, when I learned the reason things sound the way they do is because of the mathematics of music. That's when it really clicked—"Oh!"

Beautiful music is about tension and release. My favorite bands were the ones who grasped this and were always searching for new combinations and permutations to heighten the listener's experience. The Beatles, for example, would travel miles just to go to a record store because they heard so-and-so had a new record and there was this weird chord that no one knew what it was. So they'd take their guitars and they'd 'shed it (that is, woodshed it—practicing a piece or a chord) until they finally figured out, "Okay, that's why the chord sounds like it does." And between my listening to records and 'shedding the stuff on my own, and now the theory courses, it was like the whole world of music—the *hows* and *whys* for the ways certain things went together—was unfolding for me. Maybe it was a minor four chord or it contained a half-diminished note, but I'd learn it and where it fit and it was like, "Wow, that's cool." It made sense, and most importantly, I liked keeping track of it all and would *never* forget it. It was so stimulating. Maybe it's the same way some people like to do crossword or sudoku puzzles. It was like counting steps: 1, 2, 3, 4.

Subtract this, add this, substitute this. A whole world of specific but endless combinations.

When it came to my fourth-period class, school band rehearsal, my main instrument was saxophone. There were guys who were much better saxophone players, and I'd be listening to them practice in the hallways and stuff.[1] It was insane. Some of the saxophone kids in school were practicing and 'shedding stuff like "Giant Steps" by John Coltrane or something by Charlie Parker. It was cool, but I sure as hell didn't want to be just a saxophonist. I played guitar, keyboards, I sang. I was gonna be the next John Lennon. The next Jimi Hendrix. That's what I wanted to be.

Back in the '60s, kids were either a hitter, a jock, or a hippie. If you were a hitter, all you wanted to do was beat the shit out of somebody because you were in a gang. If you were a jock, then all you cared about were sports. If you were a hippie, then all you cared about was tuning out. Performing Arts was different; you weren't confined by those stereotypes. You could be yourself 100 percent of the time. Whatever that was, was accepted. Some of my best friends were gay, and we hung out and I never once felt put off; my parents knew I had gay friends because of the artistic thing about it and everybody just accepted everybody, which is something that you didn't see in most situations back then. But PA in Manhattan was a funky freak show. It was fitting in by falling out. And I fell out really good. My hair was real long, my clothes were tight. And I dug it. That's the other thing—I wasn't trying to do anything. I was being myself.

---

1. For instance, Bob Berg, who had his own solo career but also played sideman for the likes of Miles Davis, Chick Corea, Horace Silver, Dizzy Gillespie, B. B. King, and many, many more.

There wasn't even a gymnasium in the school, because it was located in an old post office. (This was way before PA went to Lincoln Center; this was its location on Forty-Sixth Street between Sixth and Seventh Avenue in Manhattan.) They set up the dance classes, with all the big bars and mirrors, in this huge area where they used to sort out the mail. Then they set up the band room on the top floor, because it was big enough for the symphonic band to meet up there. And all these different offices, sixteen-by-sixteen-foot rooms, where they put four pianos or they made up a theory class, had been rooms in the post office— that's all.

So, the old post office became a sanctuary for young artists. You'd walk down the street, or come out of school, and you'd see freaks and everybody else hanging out. It was like this great time: tie dye, a lot of fringe jackets and color, long hair, dope, and no one ever gave you a hard time. Everybody had these dreams, and everyone supported the other person's dreams, and you had this school pride of, "Yeah, this is what we do." There were obviously the ego trippers and people thinking they were better than everyone else, but you didn't hang out with those dickheads. You were smart enough not to deal with their shit because everyone else gave you encouragement. Especially the teachers: they pushed us and didn't allow us to do anything less than our best.

Kids used to smoke right in front of the school, and no one ever said anything. I don't think the teachers felt that they knew any better than the kids; they didn't come off with some authoritative posture, because these teachers were gifted musicians and they loved it. And I think the thing that really turned them on was they got to meet and know folks who they thought were going to become really creative people in the future. And indeed, a lot of us went on to do some great things. Freddie Prinze was in the grade behind me,[2] and there were a couple of great sax players. Unfortunately, a few passed away far too young. But these great teachers weren't working at some high school where the kids would rather have knitting needles in their eyes than listen to the bullshit lesson plan. These kids wanted to be there, and these teachers wanted to teach them. We had great synergy.

---

2. Freddie Prinze was an absolute phenom, and a fellow half-Rican. He dropped out of school before his senior year to be a stand-up comedian and actor, and he rose to fame with his TV show, *Chico and the Man*. Freddie unfortunately took his own life at the age of 22.

7

ESCAPE

The news that Martin Luther King had been shot and killed shook my father to his core. Until then, I didn't think anything, no matter how horrible, could do that. Such was my faith in my father's brightly shining optimism. But on that night, the light grew dark.

We'd just finished dinner and were going to watch some TV when the report came on the screen. It's one thing to not talk because you want to hear what the newsman has to say, but it's another to feel like everybody's breath has been stolen—like no one can talk, including your father. I was fifteen years old, and I remember my little sister, who was ten years younger, asking him what had happened, and he tried his best to answer, but you could see the hope draining out. It was almost like a germ or a disease had permeated the sanctuary of our little Brooklyn home, and although my father's cheer would return, we'd witnessed its vulnerability.

My good friend and fellow native New Yorker Jimmy Bralower, a producer and drum programmer who's my age and has worked with everyone from Madonna and Duran Duran to Cyndi Lauper and Mick Jagger, says that being a kid in America during the 1960s required some insulation; otherwise, you'd go crazy.[1] Because the world had gone crazy. Vietnam, assassinations, extreme civil unrest and violence . . . For many of us kids, rock 'n' roll was a refuge. We were drawn to this expansive music scene that included Richie Havens's folk music, Santana, Joan Baez, and, of course, the Beatles and Hendrix—not only because we thought it was groovy but also because we needed some emotional space—some oxygen—so we could grow as human beings. Otherwise, we would have spiritually suffocated. A lot of adults probably thought rock 'n' roll was the voice of juvenile delinquency, if not the devil. But for kids like Jimmy and me, it was salvation, proof that humanity could still create and inspire, not just belittle, taunt, humiliate, persecute, and destroy.

■ Brooklyn, 1967–1968

St. Catharine of Alexandria's Church on Forty-First Street and Fort Hamilton Parkway would usually host the Battle of the Bands. These were Friday night big deals. The local bands would come and set up their gear in the church basement, and the rest of the junior high and high schoolers would flock to the show. The church charged a dollar admission toward the collection plate and the bands would play for trophies—*tiny* trophies for first and second place that probably cost a couple bucks, and a third-place prize that was a lame stamp that said "Battle of the Bands." It was all probably just a fundraiser to pay for the monsignor's new Cadillac or something, but the crowd had a good time dancing, and the winning band got bragging rights plus a potential booking to open for a legitimate act.

---

1. Jimmy Bralower is one of my oldest and dearest friends. He and I played on Peter Gabriel's album *So* together, as well as with Hall & Oates and Billy Joel. To this day, we live just a short drive away from each other and still jam in his incredible home studio.

There would be five or six bands, and each band got to perform about a half-dozen songs. Generally, the crappiest band would open and the best band would finish. When Maitrex Square first started doing Battle of the Bands, we fell in the middle of the pack. Between all the rehearsals at the Chinese laundromat and playing for Fat Jerry's friends during their basement parties, we were now beyond the stage of simply feeling our way, pulling off songs like Hendrix's "You Got Me Floatin'" and Parliament's "Testify." Some renditions were better than others,[2] but we had a good sound, adding a bass player and keyboardist to the mix. But we were still just kids—fifteen-year-olds, except for Vinny, who was older—with no real transportation. I remember lugging our stuff, rolling our amps on dollies to go from Eighth Avenue between Forty-First and Forty-Second Street to Tenth Ave. and Fortieth Street, beneath the elevated train, making our way to the church, the promise of the Battle's big crowd more than enough to get us out the door.

Battle of the Bands was also a good opportunity to check out what other bands were doing: everything from their set list and how they played to what they wore and, perhaps most importantly, how they interacted with the crowd. Because anything to get the audience—which could be two hundred strong—digging your set was a decided edge.

This one time, we were probably the third band, and I'd dressed to kill with a black fake-fur coat, white pants, and orange socks. We ran out onto the stage, and I started our set with "Hi, y'all!" because I'd seen Mick Jagger do that in one of the Rolling Stones'

---

2. We did a particularly decent job on the tune "Omaha" by Moby Grape, which has to go down as one of the most underappreciated bands of that era. Their eponymous album *Moby Grape*—another album released in 1967, proving that it was the year in rock history—is especially good, rising to #24 on the Billboard charts.

films, and we went into Jeff Beck's "Rock My Plimsoul."[3] With our two guitars, loud and full of attitude, and the British-blues song choice, it really got the crowd going. Our entire set kicked ass, and I remember thinking we nailed it. We were definitely better than the first two bands, and we had a shot at the title.

But then the remaining bands came on, and each one was better than the next. The first was Crystal Ship. Their lead singer looked just like Jim Morrison, and they had a black light with some cool psychedelic painting as a backdrop. I can't remember what songs they played, but the combination of the lead singer's charisma with the black light and art was enough to make you stop and go, "*Whoa*," and you could feel the crowd going deeper into the music with each song.

The last band, Formula 44, was even better. Their drummer and lead singer was a kid named John Guarneri, who was a couple years older and who fucking torched the drums, bringing a sonic power into that church basement that was on another level. The crowd felt each hit in their bones as they danced around the hall. Formula 44 also had a strobe light and a fog machine, along with an organ player who played a Hammond B-3, which is like a piece of furniture and weighs about a billion pounds. He would do all these moves, like a gymnast hopping around a pommel horse, his hands pressing into the keys as his legs kicked way up in the air, into the fog, the strobe lights flickering behind him, and this kid was suddenly a rock god—all the girls, their mouths agape, watching him up onstage—catching air, frame by frame in the pulsing strobe as he ripped solos on his B-3. It was awesome. It was also

---

3. For those unfamiliar with "Rock My Plimsoul," seek it out. It's a standard 1-4-5 blues tune except you've got guitar god Jeff Beck leading a band with a young and pitch-perfect Rod Stewart on the microphone. Raw, recorded live, and as good as it gets.

deflating. They were the best band to begin with, but that strobe light and fog machine made it no contest.

Shortly after that show, I got a black light of my own, and my parents let me have a space in the basement. I painted the walls flat black and then all this groovy stuff with Day-Glo paint—it was like a little hippie den. And I brought in some speakers and a stereo; it wasn't as good as my father's but still good enough. Also I had my piano, sax, guitar, and a tiny 15-watt amp. I eventually even got a strobe light. So, unless my grandparents were down there making wine or tomato sauce, it was like my own club. You'd turn the lights off, plug in the strobe, black light, and speakers, and trip out.

Drugs were also becoming a bigger part of the whole thing. During that same Battle of the Bands, the lead singer of Crystal Ship, the one who looked like Jim Morrison, had advertised his girl-friend's mescaline for sale. "Buy Maggie's mesc," he announced a few times during the show, and the crowd would laugh. And though my friends and I didn't buy any then, a few weeks later someone got their hands on some and we headed to Sunset Park to just stroll around and see what the hell this stuff did.

As tiny as the little purple pill was, I was scared, so I only took a half. It was more of a body thing than anything, not a total hallu-cination. But it was enough to make me understand I was moving outside of my comfort zone, beyond reality, and allowing some-thing else to take control. We did it again a few weeks later, at a bit higher dose. Like watching someone step outside in a snowstorm naked, you'd say to yourself, "Now, who would think that's a good idea?" But then the other part of your brain would go, "Well, you don't know until you try."

8

THE FIREMAN

My Italian grandmother wanted me to be a fireman. Starting around my junior year of high school, she began to put the screws on me about "my future." She'd never given me a hard time about all the rock 'n' roll—the loud stereo and amps and the long hair—but now she was wondering where it was all leading. One of her other grandsons, Vincent Louis (so, one more Cousin Vinny), was already a lieutenant in the fire department, and she'd say, "Why-a-you no-a-want to be a-like your cousin?" Like most first-generation Americans starting from scratch, my grandmother thought the best job was a secure job. So, she suggested being a fireman, or if I didn't like heights, a sanitation worker, saying, "The garbage is a-dirty but the money she's a-clean."

First-generation American or not, she had a point. A career in music—like any other art form—is very often an exercise of banging your head against the wall, which of course pays nothing. And she knew me well—I mean I'd lived in the same house with her my whole life. She'd seen all of my weird childhood quirks— the blinking, the toe dragging, the counting steps—and probably deduced my craving for dependable routines. Again, consistency.

I mean pretty much every day, that same little boy would run up the fourteen steps to her apartment, and she would answer the door. Because she was always cooking, her eyeglasses would be caked full of flour. And that little boy would take the glasses and clean them, and say, "Can you see me now?"

And she'd say, "Yeah, you're such a good boy." And then ask, "Eh, Markey, you a-want a nice cup of brown coffee?" (Brown coffee meant coffee with milk.)

And the boy would say, "No, Grandma, you know I don't drink coffee." It would be the same thing over and over, like a scene in a script.

And now that little boy was running around playing music every night, and she probably thought, *This might not be the best fit for him.*

It had taken us a while to get our feet wet, but certainly by 1969, Maitrex Square was winning some Battles of the Bands. We even got to open for the Spencer Davis Group (post–Steve Winwood, unfortunately.) But then it was like, "What's next?" I understood we weren't top tier. I was the best person in the band—I could play drums as well as the drummer, I played guitar better than the guitar players, and I could sing my ass off. And look, I loved my cousin Vinny to death—I looked up to him, and he was older, smarter, and hilarious—but he wasn't a great guitarist, and I wanted to be surrounded by great musicians.

So, for my junior and senior years of high school, I started to cycle through different bands and different players. I met this girl Valerie at Performing Arts in Manhattan and spent a lot of time at her house in Queens, and there was this drummer, Adolfo, who lived next door, and then he introduced me to this guitar player who was fucking great, and I wanted to be in a band with him. And when that got tired, I wanted to be in the band with the next guy.

It was a matter of upping the game, branching out. Networking. Eventually, I started hanging at this one place we called the Loft. It was this guy Frank's place on Twenty-Second Street in Chelsea. Frank was a drug dealer and word was he supplied Jimi Hendrix when he was in the city. It was a nice setup—*two floors*—and the whole downstairs was one big hang area. People would stop by and jam, and it became this little enclave for different musicians who wanted to start new projects or just hang and make a lot of noise.

I was definitely branching out. But it caused a lot of tension. You have guys who you loved and who loved you, and suddenly, it was, "Mark, what a scumbag. He's in another band." It's like breaking up with a girlfriend because you found a hotter girl. You have to be prepared to take the assault from people who look at you like you're being a shit. Because it was true; you *were* being a shit, at least in their eyes, because no one likes to get broken up with. It isn't a nice feeling, and I hated causing people pain. But nothing was going to stop me from getting to where I needed to go.

Including school. At a certain point in time, the most important thing to me wasn't about band or theory classes—it was about learning the new Hendrix song, or a great new Beatles hit. And by now I was proficient enough to apply what I'd heard to the instrument in short order. My ears were wide open, and what they heard translated to my fingers. It didn't matter the instrument. And, again, if I hear it, I don't forget it—my brain just retains all of that stuff. So, I was learning, but according to my own syllabus.

By twelfth grade, I was already going out and playing at night, and I was missing my morning classes. So, Performing Arts gave me a choice: I had to go to night school or repeat another year; otherwise they'd give me the boot. Well, there was no way I was going to do an extra year, and the night school was a no-go because I was gigging, so they threw me out, and I spent the last half of my senior year at the local high school. I took typing and whatever bullshit classes to get a regular diploma. But I never made it to graduation day. I was in a band—the perfect band—and we were heading to Minneapolis. We'd gotten our big break.

■ ■ ■

Every band you're in, there's a piece of you that thinks, "This is gonna be the one," meaning, "this is the one that's going to get signed by a record company and we're gonna do a world tour and be on every radio station in America." And at some point, you realize that what you thought might happen is probably not going to happen and you move on. After leaving Maitrex Square and getting more selective with the players I was hanging with, I'd been in at least five serious bands—Pecker Frost, Jam Band, Tulsa, Truth, and Straight Jacket—either singing or playing whatever instrument the band needed: sax, flute, guitars, keyboards, percussion. And in each of those bands, I'd played alongside some killer musicians—guys like John Guarneri, the drummer for Formula 44 and Sir Lord Baltimore; and Carmine Rojas, an amazing bassist who would go on to play with Rod Stewart and David Bowie.

But it wasn't until I was asked to be the lead singer of Eclipse that every ounce of my being was convinced, "This is gonna be the one." The seven-piece band was full of heavy hitters, all in their twenties with a shitload of experience. The drummer had a regular gig with James Brown, the trumpet player and sax player were in the band Ten Wheel Drive,[1] and the trombone player and

---

1. While never quite reaching mainstream success, Ten Wheel Drive were known for their high-octane live shows. I recommend seeking out "The Night I Got Out of Jail" to dip your toes into what they were all about. Worth a google.

bass player were in the Mothers of Invention.[2] That's how deep this band was. And for me, the all-star was the guitarist, Kenny Papa. Two years older, Kenny was my idol. He was from Brooklyn, the real rock god of the neighborhood. Back when I was still with Vinny and Maitrex Square, Kenny was already recording with a band called Frog and they were absolute monsters. They should have had a record deal, but it had fallen through. And now Kenny had formed Eclipse with these other serious cats, and they wanted me, the kid still in high school, to be out front. It was a giant leap for me.

And the next thing I knew, I was walking on the moon. The whole band was. Because the trumpet player, Mike Lawrence, who was an absolute beast, was buddies with Lew Soloff, the trumpet player for Blood, Sweat & Tears, who stopped by the Loft to check us out and thought we sounded fucking great. So, he scored us an audition with Blood, Sweat & Tears' manager, this guy Larry Goldblatt, and Larry obviously liked what he heard, because he immediately cut us a check for $50,000 along with plane tickets and instructions to get our asses to Minneapolis for a series of gigs he'd lined up.

It all happened so fast. We did the audition on, like, a Monday, got the check on a Wednesday, and the first show was scheduled for that coming Saturday. I mean, I hadn't been with the band for six months and suddenly we were jet-setting to a huge gig backed by the manager for one of the biggest bands on the planet. Shit, two years earlier, Blood, Sweat & Tears had to be helicoptered into Woodstock by the National Guard to ensure that the six hundred thousand people who'd gathered to hear some live music didn't riot. And the guy who was in that band's corner was now in ours.

---

2. If Salvador Dalí had a rock-jazz-fusion band, then it might've come close to what the Mothers of Invention created on a daily basis.

He was going to make it all happen for us. And to think, Grandma wanted me to be a fireman . . .

So, I immediately left school, two weeks early. Didn't know if I'd graduate; didn't give a rat's ass. Life was about to change.

Starting with my wardrobe. The coolest clothes that I had were not very cool. Maybe a "fancy" shirt and a couple pairs of jeans. I still didn't have the freakin' Beatles boots. I don't even know if I thought to pack a razor. I was so unprepared. And even without much of a wardrobe, I still managed to have the world's bulkiest, big-ass suitcase, which I of course needed to borrow from my father. But it didn't matter. As far as I was concerned, this time next month I was gonna be decked out in the coolest shit, with eight pairs of Beatles boots. *Why?* Because we had a big-time manager, and he was gonna make it all happen.

And then we were on the plane. The seven of us. The first time I was on a plane to do a gig, because everything up until then for me was just a drive out to Queens, or maybe two shows out in Jersey or Long Island. But now the stewardess is bringing drinks and I'm thinking, "Wow, this is what it must have been like to be the Beatles." I can't remember if we had first class or no class, but what did it matter? We were going to be in the front of the plane soon enough. Shit, we'd probably own the plane. Why? *Because we had a big fucking manager.*

And when we got to play the gig—this place called George's in the Park near downtown Minneapolis—the band that opened for us was incredible. But they were a cover band, playing Chicago tunes. They sounded exactly like the Chicago records and the lead singer had one of those Peter Cetera tenor voices, really bright, and I was like, "Wow, these guys are good," because anytime I was in a cover band, it was more like a hand grenade as opposed to a laser. But then *we* got up and played our songs—*original* songs with titles like "Help Us" and "I'm Gonna Get You When Your

Momma's Not Around"—and that same cover band whose stellar performance had given me a little pause, who'd made me feel a bit of self-doubt, like maybe my shit wasn't good enough, was now staring up at us like, "Whoa, who's this smokin' band?" And we *were* a fucking smokin' band.

Right up until the next morning, when we got a phone call saying that Larry Goldblatt had been arrested for embezzlement. And everything, starting with the $50K right up to the private jet, went *poof!* It was gone and we all knew we were back at square one and a thousand miles away from home.

Man, it was terrible. We still committed to the next weekend's gigs, and I think I met some girl and ended up staying at somebody's apartment because it was such a drag to be at the hotel. I didn't want to be around anything. Because we were fucked. The whole band understood. This was our shot. We'd been rehearsing three days a week for six months, pouring money into rehearsal studio time. We had never even done a gig until we went to George's in the Park. Instead, we shot for the moon, only to be cut off before reaching orbit, and fell back to Earth.

Faster than a fireman down a firepole.

9

INFECTIOUS

I hardly ever do wedding gigs. But it happens. You're between tours and money is tight. So, it was one of those times and a buddy, Paul Adamy (New York Philharmonic, Todd Rundgren, Steve Jordan), put this ass-kicking band together for the gig. That's the thing: whether you're playing Madison Square Garden or a ballroom at the Plaza, a good jam is a good jam. And when you're in the middle of that, I don't care what's going on, life is good.

So we play the set, and the drummer, this cat Clint De Ganon, who I'd never teamed up with before, says, "Jesus, man. You're Mr. I.V.!"

And I said, "What's an I.V.?"

And Clint goes, "Infectious Vibe, man! And I'm digging it!"

Clint's been around. He's manned the throne on hundreds of records and toured with the likes of Randy Jackson, Will Lee, and Stevie Wonder. He knows when guys are bringing their A-game. He also knows when someone's just going through the motions.

When I'm onstage, I don't simply show up. I'm totally enthralled and enjoying every moment of that performance.

Because *music* is infectious. There's something about that ebb and flow between tension and release that gets me going. I guess I could put the brakes on and not allow myself to go there, but why deny myself the pleasure? Again, *don't just eat the peach— let it run down your chin.*

And whether you're behind the kit or up in the nosebleeds, you can't help but get swept up in that sort of enthusiasm. I think it's why guys like Billy and Ringo hire players like me. Sure, we can blow and bang on shit and make a good sound, but so can lots of people. There's got to be something more, another dimension, so that when the front man needs someone to take the spotlight for a little bit, he's got it; or if he yells "All right!" or "Here we go!" there's another gear, a few more notches.

After that craziness went down in Minneapolis, Eclipse scattered to the wind. So-and-so went here and so-and-so went there. Everyone had other serious projects and gigs to roll into, but I didn't. And while I'm sure the whole ordeal hurt them, they were older than me, wiser, and more calloused. They understood that this business is largely about getting screwed, and somewhere in the back of their minds, they probably thought it would still most likely go to pot. But I was blindsided. We'd even come up with the idea for our first album cover, sketching it out on the plane ride to Minneapolis—the word "Eclipse," eclipsing the sun, eclipsing the moon (I know, mind-blowing).

But it's not like I came away empty. Ultimately, I had more swagger, confidence—whatever it is that people want to see on a stage, I had. Maybe it wasn't completely honed, but it was there. I mean, I was *chosen* to be in a band by Kenny Papa, the Brooklyn phenom whom I idolized. Yeah, so we didn't make the big time—and that took a while to get over, especially with my grandmother doubling down on her yakking about becoming a fireman or a garbageman—but some real cats had given me their seal of approval. Why? Simple: I had the I.V., man! The Infectious Vibe. And for the next couple of years, I just kept my head down, playing in NYC bands, making some dough, honing my craft. The dream wasn't realized but it was very much alive.

■ New York City, 1974

Marty Castori was a year younger and lived in Brooklyn, on Tehama Street, right around the corner from my girlfriend's apartment. We'd started hanging, jamming in his parents' basement, and Marty, who is this killer guitar player—he has this sort of Buzzy Feiten style—was really into modal jazz.[1] So he'd be on his guitar, and I'd play mostly saxophone, and we were both stretching ourselves a bit musically, 'shedding some heavy stuff like Herbie Hancock's "Maiden Voyage," opening our ears to a whole new complexity of music. Anyway, Marty played with a lot of acts around the city and had already spent a summer touring with the duo Sam & Dave. That was a big-time gig.

Sam & Dave, a.k.a. Double Dynamite and The Sultans of Sweat, were one of the most successful acts of the '60s. If you've seen the movie *The Blues Brothers*, you know their music. Tracks like "Soul Man," "Hold On, I'm Comin'," and "I Thank You." They were huge, smash hits, and only Aretha Franklin, the Queen of Soul, did more to put soul music on the national stage.[2]

---

1. Howard "Buzz" Feiten is a local legend and is probably best known for playing with the likes of Bob Dylan, Aretha Franklin, Stevie Wonder, James Taylor, Etta James, Gregg Allman, and so many more.

2. *Rolling Stone* has a pretty solid Top 20 ranking for Greatest Duos of All Time. Sam & Dave come in at #14, just ahead of Steely Dan. (https://www.rollingstone.com/music/music-lists/20-greatest-duos-of-all-time-16272/20-the-black-keys-67774/)

So, we were jamming one day, and Marty said that he was going back out on the road with the trailblazing duo as a member of the band.

"They're looking for a sax man," Marty said.

"No shit?" I asked, trying my best to remain cool. A gig like Sam & Dave was a national tour, which sounded like a hell of a better way to spend the summer than sweating cover-band gigs in the city.

"Yeah, I told them I might know a guy," Marty smiled—New York Italians are nothing if they don't know how to take the piss out of one another.

"Oh yeah? Who'd you recommend?" I asked.

A week or so later, the band invited me to rehearsal.

So, Marty and I get to the rehearsal and the backing band is there. (Not Sam and Dave, of course, who were the front men.) It's a seven-piece setup—drums, bass, guitar, and horns—and the whole cast except for Marty is Black and super laid-back. I mean these dudes were like plasma, in no rush to go through the set. Everything was like, "Yeah, we'll get to it, it's chill," which was very different from other tryouts or rehearsals I'd been in where guys were a lot more wired up and ready to go. And the musical director, Ben Little, who was also the trombone player, goes, "Hey man, you wanna join this band? You gotta get deep in the pocket, like down in the lint."

So, I said, "Okay, I can dig it," and eventually things got rolling.

Right from the first measure, I understood that in order to play with this band and not stick out like a sore thumb, I had to adjust my body clock. As Ben said, I had to "get deep in the pocket." Because in music there's some flexibility to the notes written on the page. *There's space for feel.* And that feel—whether you're looking to hustle or lay back—really happens on the non-dominant beats. What we call the backbeat. (So, if you're playing something in 4/4 time, meaning four beats per measure, then the non-dominant beats are the 2 and the 4; conversely, the 1 and the 3 are the dominant beats.) And these cats were riding way back on the backbeat—deep in the pocket—creating these irresistible, soulful grooves.

So, we went through the set and I felt solid. I'd been able to practice the material with Marty the day before, and, besides, I already knew the songs. It was all the same stuff I'd been playing with Maitrex Square and at those basement parties Fat Jerry had lined up for us.

So then Ben Little goes, "Say man, you blow bari?" asking me if I play the baritone sax.

And I'm like, "Yeah man, I play bari."

And Little says, "Cool, man. Bring your bari tomorrow to rehearsal."

So, I say, "Yeah, cool."

Marty and I head back to Brooklyn, and Marty goes, "You've never played the baritone sax in your life, have you?"

And I told him, "That's right," because the only saxophone I'd strapped on up to that point was an alto. So, I went home and I got my father to give me the $100 to rent a baritone sax and a mouthpiece from Pontes Music in Manhattan. I rented the sax and went back home and I'm 'shedding this thing for about six hours. I was about 130 pounds at the time and the baritone was about a third of that. So I'm playing and playing, wrestling this huge-ass instrument but feeling more comfortable as I go because, fortunately, the alto and baritone are both in E-flat and it's the same fingering and register.

The next day arrives, and I play the baritone saxophone in this horn section, and I fucking nailed it. So I'm thinking, *Oh, I definitely got the gig*, but then Ben Little goes, "Cool, man. Now you gotta learn the steps."

And I'm like, *Oh shit, the steps.* Because, of course, a band this cool couldn't have a horn section that just stood still. (I mean, we're not talking *The Lawrence Welk Show* here, people.) So, Ben shows me the steps where I bend down with the sax and the trumpet player goes right across my head with his trumpet. Then the trumpets go to the right, and I go back up . . . So now I'm playing, Mr. Italian–Puerto Rican Stringbean, with this monster baritone sax and I'm bobbin' and weavin'—*down, up, down, up, to the left, to the right*—choreographed with the rest of the horn section. Fortunately for my teeth, I got the sequence down and never miscued.

And it was a blast. Shit, man, it's *soul* music.

10

LADIES AND GENTLEMEN, PLEASE REMAIN CALM

■ **Brewster, New York, 2020**

My doctor recently asked me about my consumption habits. He knew that my father died from diabetes and wanted to know what crap I was putting into my body.

"Well," I said. "I love a glass of milk and a black-and-white cookie before bed."

And he looked at me with real concern, and said, "Mark, black-and-white cookies are poison to you."

And I'm like, Oh, shit, because I really like them.

So, I told him how healthy I was—I exercise, eat a shitload of vegetables, and hadn't done any hard drugs in more than a dozen years. I mean, I'd rather piss in a bowl of cocaine than take a hit.

But he was adamant, saying the sugar and the milk were the last things my body needed.

So, I stopped. I still sneak a couple of oatmeal cookies now and then, but I quit drinking milk, which was the hardest part.

It's funny how we have these little bargains with God—"I'll do this, dear Lord, if you wouldn't mind letting me stick around a bit longer." And I genuinely thank God for the time he's given me. I say my prayers before bed, trying not to ask for anything but just praying for others and expressing gratitude for the gifts I've been given. Maybe it goes back to my compulsiveness as a kid to always make things even and balanced, so my universe would stay upright. But I do it every night and I'm still here—still upright.

But for a period of time, my late teens through mid-twenties, I'd actually become fatalistic about death—*it doesn't matter what I do, I'm gonna die.* Sure, at a certain level, everyone knows they're gonna die, but I was convinced that I was gonna die and I was gonna die young. In fact, I even knew the date: *7/13/77.* There was something about the way the digits lined up that clicked inside my brain (that other childhood compulsion—numbers—or maybe it's all part of the same thing).

I can't explain it because there's nothing rational about thinking you're gonna die on a specific date. But it was there, not front and center, but like a billboard up the road. Your brain doesn't even register it. But at the same time, it does, and in my case, even though it was still too far away to read, I somehow knew what the billboard said: *Mark Dies Now.*

Again, I can't explain it.

■ New York City, 1974

The day after I got the gig with Sam & Dave, we did a full rehearsal, and Sam and Dave were there. I'd be lying if I said I remember the specific moment we were introduced, but I'm sure they noticed their backing band had picked up another white dude, this one in the horn section. What I do remember from that rehearsal is that Sam was in charge. It was clearly his band, not Dave's. It was also obvious that Sam and Dave didn't talk much to each other. They seemed to avoid even looking in the other's general direction. It struck me as odd because I'd never been in a band that could suffer bad blood for any length of time. It would just break up and everyone would go their own way. But these guys, Sam and Dave, had been at it a long time and were about to head out on tour. *How's this gonna work?*

Two days later, we were in Central Park, opening for Ray Charles at the Schaefer Music Festival. It was our warmup before hitting the road the next morning.

So, we're in the park and we finish soundcheck, and everybody goes off and does their thing while Ray Charles and his guys do their soundcheck. An hour later, it's time to hit it and we reconvene backstage. Everyone except Ben Little.

Anyone seen Ben? We're on in fifteen minutes.

Nope.

Then, it's five minutes.

Where's Ben?

Then we're on stage. We do the entire set. Ben never shows.

And I remember feeling a bit let down, like some of the shine had been scuffed away. I'd never played on a stage this big before or for a band that had actual songs on the radio. And yeah, Sam & Dave were a decade beyond their prime, and yeah, we're just the opening act, but it was a huge deal for me. And while I was having a blast, blowing my bari, doin' the steps, in the back of my mind, I was sort of like, *Well, that's a bummer—our MD didn't show.*

So, we wrap, and now Ray Charles and his band are on stage. Sam and Dave are long gone but the rest of us are hanging out offstage watching the great Ray Charles perform. And Ray's sitting at the piano, deep into the keys and singing his ass off, when his valet—the guy who escorts Ray on and off stage—walks up to him and whispers something into Ray's ear. And Ray, mid-phrase, stops performing, takes the valet's arm, and calmly walks off the stage. Meanwhile, his band is still going.

So, we're still watching from the wings, wondering *what the fuck*, when the sound cuts and an announcement comes over the PA system:

"Ladies and gentlemen, there's been a power failure. Please remain calm as we sort the technical issue."

Or something to that effect. But whatever it was, it didn't make any sense—you don't "whisk" Ray Charles away for a power outage, and besides, why were the guys' amps still powered on and the stage lights beaming down? Unlike the PA system, none of that would be hooked to an emergency generator. Something else was up.

Then we got word from someone backstage that the "technical issue" was actually a bomb threat, and the bit about the power outage was just to avoid panic.[1] Now the PA announcer was telling the crowd that Ray Charles was ill, the concert rescheduled, and to please vacate the premises.

I can't remember who said it first, but some of my bandmates assumed that Ben, our missing music director/trombonist, called in the bomb threat. Apparently, Ben was a heroin addict, and they deduced he'd probably had a little more than he could handle after the soundcheck, passed out, and woke up in a panic,

---

1. The full report from the *New York Times* on August 20, 1974: "A bomb threat last night cut short the Ray Charles Show at the Schaefer Music Festival in Central Park, causing Mr. Charles, who is blind, to be led off the stage after only four songs.

"In an apparent effort to avert a panic, it was first announced by Ron Delsener, producer of the series, that there had been a power failure. Then it was announced that Mr. Charles was ill and that the show would be rescheduled.

"After the capacity audience of 6,000 had filed out of the Wollman Skating Rink Theater, the Central Park precinct reported that an unidentified caller had informed Police Headquarters that a bomb had been hidden under the bandshell, forcing the interruption. No bomb was found, the police said."

knowing he'd cocked up. So, he called in the bomb threat as a sort of half-baked diversion. I don't know how plausible this was or if this sort of thing had happened before, but the group seemed confident in their theory. But Marty and I weren't taking any chances, and we huffed it out of Central Park. Marty lugged his hundred-pound amplifier while I carried his guitar, my alto, and of course, the big-ass baritone saxophone, scooting past the six thousand other people who had no idea they whether might blow up at any second.

It was another letdown on what should have been a fantastic experience. Still, it wasn't enough to give Marty or me cold feet. We were ready to hit the road, and the next morning, along with the rest of the band, we showed up at the Midtown rendezvous. And this time, Ben Little *was* there, but feeling no need to explain his whereabouts the previous evening. Ben was not only the music director, he was also the band's most senior member—the only one who'd been along for the ride when Sam & Dave were on top of the charts. He ruled the roost, at least when Sam was not around, which I gathered was most of the time. (For their part, Sam and Dave would be legging out the tour in style, thirty thousand feet above our heads and staying in real hotels. Apparently, there was still enough money in the cookie jar for that.)

Not that it mattered to me. I was pumped, regardless of who was in charge or what their habits were. For the first time, I was part of a touring band, and with my two saxophones and a piece of luggage, I saddled up for the journey. But instead of going south on I-95 to get to wherever we were going—Tennessee, I think—Ben steered the station wagon and U-Haul trailer with all the equipment inside north, to Harlem, so the guys could cop some methadone. Evidently, everyone but Marty and I had a fondness for the drug, along with heroin, the tragic magic that likely had detained the music director the night before.

So, we got to Harlem and waited four hours for the drug dealers to show up.

Finally, the interstate was passing beneath our tires. And I was like, *Holy shit, I'm living the dream! I don't know what's next and I don't care!* Which was good because there didn't seem to be much of a compass as to where we were going.

■ ■ ■

We started playing the shows, which were mostly halls and clubs scattered around the South, and the days sort of folded into one another. I kind of dug that about the road: we were outside the rules and norms of life that people—even musicians—assume when you're living in one place.

You're in the car forever. It's after a gig and you're half asleep, hoping the guy behind the wheel doesn't nod off and kill you. But it would be dark, and you're stoned or had a drink or whatever and you just got finished playing so you could space out, and you could be in the car for hours and not realize it. Or it's the day after and you had fun the night before. You're going a few hundred miles at a clip, the radio on and guys joking around. I remember the drummer, this guy Gregory Brown, would talk like a white guy—"Yeah, you guys talk all white"—and he'd make fun of Marty and me, and we'd give it right back and all the guys would laugh. And then you'd stop to gas up and take a leak, maybe grab a piece of fried chicken, and hit the road again for another three hundred miles.

Sometimes it wasn't so easy. Maybe it had been a rough night, and no one was really talking, and the next gig might be a thousand miles away. That's how far we'd go sometimes, like someone was throwing darts at a map, and we'd have a day and a half to get there. But even all of that was okay because we'd eventually get to where we were going and there'd be a show to play. You didn't have to worry about booking the next gig. It was already booked.

You didn't have to worry about making enough dough. You were making $500 a week, more than you'd ever made in your life. You didn't have to worry about "When am I gonna start being a real rock 'n' roller?" because you were on the road, with a real band, *being* a rock 'n' roller. There were no worries. You were crashing in dive hotels, telling jokes, playing gigs, eating at roadside diners, sleeping on the road, meeting barmaids, hanging out. It was the road and no matter what, you always had a gig at the other end of it.

And the drugs helped. Marty and I didn't go for the heroin or meth, and Marty didn't smoke much. But we'd drink and I'd smoke pot, maybe get my hands on a little bit of coke, or maybe something to take the edge off, like some type of barbiturate if that was around. If I got lucky, I'd get some good hash. I wasn't doing any acid or speed because you wouldn't want to be tripping or amped up on those long stretches of road. You just wanted things to blur, fall out of time a bit. Especially if things ever went a bit sideways.

Like when we got pulled over in Mississippi.

There were three guys who drove and one of them, the trumpet player, had a suspended license. And at some point, early on in the tour, I remember thinking this probably wasn't such a good idea, but that concern had sort of faded away. So now it's after a gig and this dude is driving, and as we're going over a bridge, lights from a police car are coming up behind us. And everyone immediately starts rolling down windows, throwing shit out. Methadone, heroin, pot, booze, any drugs we had went sailing over the bridge. And Ben Little, who'd been sleeping in the back, passes his driver's license up to the trumpet player, and I'm thinking this is really stupid because Ben is a 5'5" fat dude, and the trumpet player is about 6'6" and skinny as a rail.

So, the cop, this big Southern boy with a big ol' Southern cop hat, comes up to the driver's window and he's shining his flashlight while the trumpet player is trying to look as small as possible and none of us are looking at the cop because we're all stoned. And I don't know what it was—a busted taillight on the trailer or what—but the cop asks the trumpet player for his license. There were no pictures on licenses back then, but the cop starts asking the trumpet player's name, date of birth, and all of that and I'm thinking we're fucked, and that I can't believe we're in whatever state we're in—Mississippi or wherever—and I'm going to end up in a Southern jail with five Black guys.

But the trumpet player, whose name I can't remember, starts answering all of the questions, and he must have gotten them right because the cop let us go. So the trumpet player had obviously memorized the information ahead of time and saved our ass. So anyway, imagine doing speed or trippin' with that shit going on. I'd have probably jumped off the bridge.

And even when we weren't doing something that stupid, there would always be a little sense of danger or insecurity. Because seven Black guys and two white guys touring through the South together didn't exactly afford peace of mind. A lot of Southerners made their views on race and race mixing pretty obvious. A white boy on stage with a bunch of Black boys? *Shame on you.* It wasn't everyone, but there'd always be some club owner with a scowl or fans in the audience with a sudden hitch in their dance step. They'd be grooving, smiling up at the band, and then they'd see me or Marty and sort of freeze, like it didn't compute. And then, when it did—*Oh, he's white*—there'd be a frown or a shaking of the head. Marty would just keep wailing his guitar and I'd keep blowing my horn, doin' the steps, and fortunately, those people would fold right back into the music, too caught up in the bass and drums and those two men belting it out than to let whatever other emotions were tugging at them win them over.

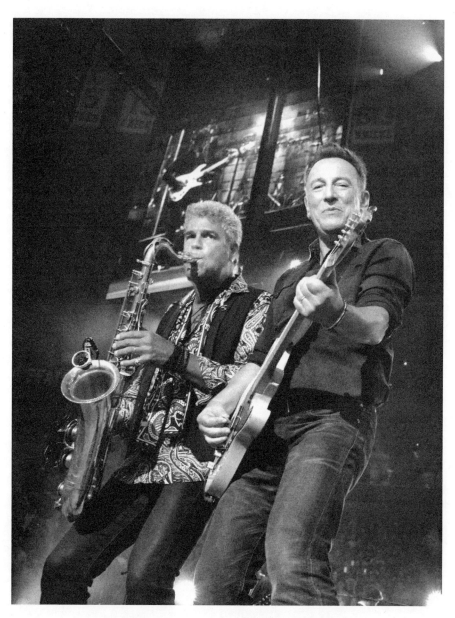

Rocking "Born to Run" with surprise guest Bruce
Springsteen at Billy Joel's 100th career MSG
show. July 18, 2018. (Credit: Myrna Suárez)

11

CHUGALUG

Looking back, when I was on the road with Sam & Dave, it was totally the minor leagues. As a duo, Sam & Dave were on the back side of their careers, and with the exception of the drummer, Greg Brown (who performed with Stevie Wonder), the rest of the band were really just double-A players. Some of us were possibly on the way up, hopeful to one day play the big shows in the big stadiums with the big crowds. I know that was very much on my radar. But I was young and dumb, and probably, like a minor-league player climbing the baseball chain, I failed to understand how hard the grind of the road and the loss of attention must've been for the guys on their way down. Dave most of all. While Sam had this resilient energy to match his big smile and beautiful high voice, Dave would get dark and brooding.

One time, it was early in the tour, we'd just finished a show and the manager was paying us our cut, and Dave asked me if I'd ever shot craps. He'd rightly pegged me, the new guy, as an easy target. So, we shot craps and as luck would have it, I won all of Dave's money. And instead of getting on a plane the next day, the now cash-strapped Dave had to ride in the station wagon with me and the rest of his backing band. The whole trip he seemed miserable, and I remember thinking the money I'd won wasn't worth it because he was obviously pissed and kept hacking his throat and spitting whatever contents he'd exhumed into the headrest behind me. But at least he got to sit in the far back where there was a bit more leg room.

Another time, Dave got really drunk after a show. The audience had been pretty cold, and Dave was sitting up at the club's bar, sort of ranting to Marty and me. "You motherfuckers don't know. We used to have private jets. I used to have a private jet and could go wherever the hell I wanted to go." He must have said the words "private jet" twelve times in a three-minute period. And then he and Ben Little—the only member of the band who had been with the duo during the good ol' days—started reminiscing about the valets and girls and huge wardrobes full of suits. "And now we got jack shit," Dave lamented.

Knowing what I know now, fifty years later, about the road and what the different tours can afford, Dave probably had one or two carry-on bags, maybe two or three suits, stayed at a two- or three-star hotel without much of a view, and had to pay for his own room service and dry cleaning. As for the valets, he was doing all the lugging himself. So, money was obviously tight, and it just got to Dave, especially if the crowd was thin or not into it. But if the crowd was good, the music would lift him up and he'd be all right.

■ On the Road with Sam & Dave, 1974

Of course, when I joined Sam & Dave, I thought, *Well, shit, I made it. I'd made it to the big time.* But then, starting with Ben Little not showing up for the opener and the bomb scare in Central Park, that illusion started to fade bit by bit, gig by gig. At first it was easy to ignore because I was so intoxicated by the freedom of the road and the getting paid and the steady gig. But by month two, the shine had worn thin, and by month three, the shine was gone. That was around the time when the bassist, Chugalug, threatened to kill me.

"I'm gonna cut that motherfucker's heart out!" he declared from the station wagon's backseat. Evidently, I'd pissed him off after that evening's show by messing around with a barmaid he'd had his eye on. He kept saying, "This white boy thinks he can take all the white women and now I'm gonna cut 'im." I can't remember if he actually had a knife but Chugalug did have a checkered past, including time served for manslaughter. Word was he'd gotten out about six months before the tour.

It was true that I'd been somewhat successful with the ladies over the past few months, but so were a lot of the guys. Chugalug just had it out for me, the young happy-go-lucky guy with all that enthusiasm on stage. It didn't help that I happened to play his instrument, the bass, better than he did, which isn't saying much because Chugalug wasn't a great player. He simply wasn't. I would never say that to him or try to show him up, but when you're on the road, wrapping soundcheck, and one of the guys says, "Hey, Mark, let's jam!" you pick up whatever's lying around. So sometimes I'd pick up Chugalug's bass because I liked playing bass, and Marty would have his guitar and Greg Brown would start pumping out something groovy on the kit. We'd just play and have fun. It wasn't my fault if some of the other guys said, "Damn, Mark should be playing bass for this band. Fuck Chugalug."

But according to Chugalug, I'd stepped over the line and now needed to die in the middle seat of that station wagon on some backcountry road. And I remember thinking that maybe I should have gotten into some fights as a kid because I probably couldn't take Chugalug if he made a move. But he didn't; he just kept threatening.

Finally, we got to a gas station and, after filling up the tank, Ben Little went to the back trailer and started pulling shit out. I didn't know what the hell was going on, but he came back to the station wagon with Chugalug's bass and luggage and told Chugalug, "Get the fuck out of my car, man!" He fired him on the spot. I don't think any of us, including Chugalug, had any clue where we were. Probably someplace between Tennessee and Georgia. But that's the last I ever saw of Chugalug. Ben must have had someone already in mind to take the bass gig because we didn't miss a date. And $500 a week was good pay for anyone with fresh sea legs.

But I'd had enough. Soon after the ordeal with Chugalug, we finished the tour segment, and when we got back to New York, I told Ben Little I was gonna pass on the next one, that the dates and distances between gigs were getting too big. Ben understood. I wasn't exactly the first guy to go looking for something better.

Of course, the only problem was I didn't have something better to roll into. (I told you I was young and dumb.)

12

BACK TO THE CATSKILLS

■ **Brewster, New York, 2020**

It's been months since my last gig . . .

I haven't gone this long without being in front of an audience since Population 4 played its first show at Melody Lanes. Sure, I've done some virtual gigs these past few weeks. A few of us will get together and record something to video and "share" it. But that doesn't count. I mean, you can't call it a real gig if there's no one actually present in the room. Like sex, performance doesn't work that way.

For the live musician, a crowd is everything. My friend and legendary drummer Yogi Horton (Aretha Franklin, Luther Vandross, John Lennon) used to say that when the crowd is in it, everyone's head looks like a basketball, bouncing the same dribble, totally in sync. The audience is in your hand, and you're in theirs. It can be a twenty-thousand-seat venue, like that last Billy show in Mexico City, or it might be a club with a few hundred people, and you can see the joy on faces all the way to the back of the room. That'll give a musician his fix. Because when the crowd's all

77

moving the same way and everyone's digging it, being on stage is the greatest feeling in the world.

I miss that and I want it back. Everyone does.

■ South Fallsburg, New York, 1974

The only thing worse than playing to no crowd is playing for people who couldn't give a shit. (Again, not to be crude, but what's better: masturbation or having sex with someone who couldn't care less?) But that's what happens when you play Latin cocktail music, which by rule is music a person wants to turn down, not up.

It was our second night at the Raleigh Hotel, in this sort of speakeasy lounge they had called The Swizzle Stick, where patrons talked and clinked glasses at the bar and at the little tables and booths. The only person in the room who seemed to be intently listening to the music was the band leader. My cousin Vinny was right: he was an asshole, if for no other reason than the amount of schmaltz he smothered on each phrase of each terrible tune. It was unbearable, and if I hadn't smoked a joint before the hour-long set, I probably would have just taken the bass and cracked him over the head. Anything to stop all of these over-sentimental *oohs* and *aahs* and *yeahs* coming out of his mouth. *Yuck.* Where was Chugalug when you needed him to stab somebody?

But I'd put myself in this position. I'd quit Sam & Dave—cats with real soul playing real songs in front of real audiences. *Why?* I was stupid enough to think I'd just roll right into something better. But it had been months since I'd parted ways, and though I was playing gigs all over the city, it was mostly cover tunes, a lot of which were Sam & Dave songs because they were still so stuck in my head. It's a very strange thing to play a cover of the band you just departed. It makes you wish—no matter how difficult the road may have gotten—you were back on stage with the original guys.

What was I thinking, giving up that gig? I'd stupidly traded it for a spot no musician wants to be in: no steady gig at all.

So, now I'm playing these dumb bass lines, stuffed into that tuxedo, my neck all hot and scratchy beneath its collar of obedience, watching those people talk, talk, talk, and hearing the lousy lounge singer schmaltz, schmaltz, schmaltz. It was too much and making me second-guess *everything.* Like maybe Grandma was right—maybe I should become a fireman, and maybe Dad should never have taken me to the Apollo that night to see Sonny Rollins, and maybe Titi Iris should never have bought me that Beatles record, and maybe I never should have cared so much about winning the Battles of the Bands in the church basement and playing with new cats and wearing the funky clothes and all the practice, practice, practice. What good had it done me other than to land me here, in the seventh circle of hell? All of those thoughts were floating around, poking my brain, telling me, *You made a big fucking mistake.*

Thankfully, the set ended, and we got a few drinks from the bar. The band leader asked if I was having any trouble with the chord changes and I said no, which wasn't exactly true because I was really zoned out of the music and didn't know any of the fucking tunes. I could tell he was annoyed with me but also curious about what I thought about his performance, so he said it was a good set and I just nodded, probably saying something like, "Yeah man, that was great," and smiled back, trying not to be a dick, as I stared into my drink a bit too long.

Then the guys who were playing between our sets—this little jazz group—were calling me up on stage. We'd hung out some and Vinny had told them about Sam & Dave. They asked me if I wanted to sit in. And even though I was on my feet and pulling the saxophone out of the case, the half of my brain that was saying, "Cool, let's play," was being told by the other half, "Why bother?"

I can't remember how long we went or what we played. I recall the band starting up and thinking they were good and at first just listening to what they were doing and getting hip to this feeling growing inside of me, that embedded in their chords and rhythm was the cure to my woes—my task with the saxophone was to tease it out. And at some point, I remember looking up and seeing that the people in the lounge had actually stopped talking. They were watching us, tuned in, listening to music they suddenly wanted to turn up. They were no longer just people in a room. They were an audience.

When I went back to the table, there was a guy sitting next to Vinny. His name was Bob Livingood, a trumpet player with the big band that played the hotel's much larger Starlight Room. The previous evening, Vinny had dragged me to see the big band play, saying, "You gotta meet this trumpet player. He's really good."

Frankly, I wasn't that interested in the big band because I wasn't a big band guy, but the guy was a killer trumpet player with great chops. He was also a decent amount older than we were and sort of square and religious, but Vinny had gotten him high a few months before, and he became one of those "Hey, got any pot? Got any pot?" puppy-dog types.

Anyway, Bob was there after I played the set with the jazz guys and he said, "You got a great tone, buddy!" Then he told me he was part of a ten-piece band that practiced out of the Record Plant, a big-time recording studio in the city. "Come check us out sometime," he said, and I could tell he meant it.

And I remember saying "Cool" and "Thanks" and thinking *Holy shit, the Record Plant*. Located on West Forty-Fourth Street, that was where Hendrix had recorded *Electric Ladyland*. It was the first studio of its kind, a place where musicians had space to not only record but also hang and lounge, and there were multiple floors of recording rooms and rehearsal spaces. It was rock 'n' roll's haven for creativity and collaboration, and everyone who was any-one, from John Lennon and the Stones to Bowie and Aerosmith, walked its halls and spent time in its rooms.

On the drive home, Vinny and I got super stoned. The music was cranking, and we were laughing the whole way. In the coming weeks, the band leader would fire me, which wasn't a surprise and ultimately didn't matter. Because Bob Livingood, the killer trumpet player, would get in touch, and soon I'd be in his ten-piece band and basically living at the Record Plant. All of that was ahead of me. But for now, riding in my cousin's car, heading back to the neighborhood where we'd grown up together, there was just the radio and the drugs and hanging with my cousin. It had been a rotten gig. But out of that rotten gig, Vinny had gotten me up on stage playing with the jazz cats for a little soul-healing session. He'd introduced me to Bob Livingood. And even though it might not come to anything, at least I was back to feeling like I was moving forward again. I didn't know how long the feeling would last. But I was gonna ride it, however far it would carry me.

PART TWO

With Lou Gramm. Richfield, Ohio,
November 15, 1981. (Credit: Lynn Heydenreich)

13

DREAMS, AMBITION, AND OTHER OVERSIZED ITEMS

■ **Brewster, New York, 2020**

I'm cleaning out my closet.

Throughout my career, I've gathered these fancy clothes—lots of stage outfits, cool shirts or whatever. Stuff that I'd think, *Oh, that's really bitchin'*. And maybe I'd wear it. But a lot of times, I'd get home and look at it and think, *Nah, you'll never wear that*, and put it in the closet to just hang there.

And what's really been hitting home these past months is something my father used to say: "You can only wear one suit at a time." Because the truth is that I don't need all of this crap. They're just clothes. And somebody needs this stuff more than I do. And yeah, it's rock 'n' roll stuff, but maybe they have a son who could fit into these old leather pants, or maybe they'll feel a bit better because, *hey, I got a Billy Joel T-shirt*. They might not even like Billy Joel, but it's a shirt.

85

So, Sandra and I've been going to the churches or drop boxes for Vietnam veterans. Every month to six weeks, we'll take another load. And I see guys walking around with Def Leppard shirts, and I'm not sure they've ever heard a Def Leppard song in their lives. But they're wearing something that someone gave them. And that's the part of me that says, "You know, this is good. This is helpful."

Still, there are some things I haven't been able to part with.

Like years ago, on one of the first tours that I did with Billy. I'd been to London only once prior. And I was hopping around town with a guy named Dean Freidman. It must have been during the Innocent Man tour because we were doing better, and by that time, I thought I was gonna be a millionaire. Because I was already on the album cover of *An Innocent Man*, and I still had hopes of becoming a front man in my own band.

So, we go down King's Road, which is way upper-class and groovy—Barney's and stuff. And there was this clothing designer named Stephen King who was the coolest of the cool in the '80s. He was also expensive. I mean, the shirts were like $800. And there was a coat that was black and white—for a while there, everything was black and white. And the coat was maybe $1,200—way more than I could afford. But it was this huge black-and-white coat that I had to have.

Anyway, it's been about thirty-five years and I've worn the crazy coat maybe twice.

For some reason, I keep holding on to it. I don't know why. Maybe somewhere in my subconscious is the fear that I've yet to be able to attain something this cool in my career, and I have to hold on to it. But one of these days, I promise, I will give that coat away. And someone will take this coat and it'll be cold, and no one will know what the hell this person is doing, wearing this ridiculous article of clothing. It'll probably be in some Rust Belt working town, but that coat will keep this person warm and do a lot more good than just sitting in my fucking closet. (So, keep an eye out.)

But some things I will never get rid of. Like the outfit I wore when I played with John Lennon in 1975.

The gig was at the Grand Ballroom of the Waldorf Astoria in New York City. We performed three songs: Little Richard's "Slippin' and Slidin'," Ben E. King's "Stand by Me," and John's "Imagine." It was for a live BBC tribute show, *Salute to Sir Lew—The Master Showman,* an homage to British media mogul Lew Grade that went across the Atlantic. It was all done to track, like a music video. So, we weren't really performing. Just lip-synching to our prerecorded instruments. Only John's voice was live.

Anyway, Yoko wanted to use the show as an opportunity to demonstrate the level of duplicity in our government, so she designed the costumes. She made everyone in the band go see this woman who was a sculptor to make a mold of our faces. And she fashioned these skull caps, so we were each bald and had the molds of our faces on the back of our heads. The effect was like we were two-faced. It was a little bizarre. But Yoko also dressed us in these Lycra jumpsuits. Really sexy. Most of them were black paratrooper jumpsuits; John's was red.

I still have my jumpsuit. It's in my closet near the ridiculous black-and-white Stephen King jacket. But I'll hold on to the jumpsuit for the rest of my days. Because that's one of the coolest moments I've ever had on stage. Sure, it was all for show, but I was playing with John in what would ultimately be his last live performance and TV appearance.[1]

Some things are worth keeping.

---

1. Lennon's last *major* concert appearance occurred the previous year, when he appeared at Elton John's Thanksgiving performance at Madison Square Garden.

■ 1975-1978

After the gigs in the Catskills, Bob Livingood was true to his word. He got in touch, and I headed to the Record Plant to hear his band.

I wasn't there to play—just to listen—but it didn't matter. I was like a kid going into Yankee Stadium. I remember the studio lobby. I'm standing there, telling the receptionist I was invited to see the band rehearse. And it was like there was this electricity in the building. Because I knew that right beyond the doors were Studio A and Studio B and upstairs was Studio C and the cutting room. And you start to wonder, *Well, who's in there?* It might have been the Who or the Stones or John Lennon. It could have been any one of a thousand bands in there.

So, I walked into the rehearsal room and it was a nine-piece band. I'd played with the group's keyboardist, Jon Colbert (Tom Chapin, Henry Gross), in a previous band. Jon was a killer song-writer and a monster on keys. And I was salivating because, besides Jon, they had four horns, a kickass guitarist, and a great rhythm section. *All* of these guys were monsters.

They called themselves Dog Soldier, named after a John Lennon lyric. But that would soon be changed to BOMF, short for "Bunch of Mother Fuckers." And that's what these cats were: a *bunch of motherfuckers.*

A month later, they asked me to audition because they needed a new sax guy. Apparently, the previous player was a bit of a drip. He was a music teacher and a good reader, and they'd give him a chart and the dude could read it and play it. But he was kind of a flop on stage. He wore glasses and hunched over, from grading too many papers or something. It was the antithesis of what the band was trying to get people to do, which was get your groove on.

Most of the guys had never heard me play sax. But obviously I knew Bob and had hit it off with the lead singer, this guy, Patrick

Jude, who was the star of *Jesus Christ Superstar* on Broadway. And frankly, that's what's gotten me so many gigs—the energy and vibe I try to bring into the room. And I looked the part, too. I had my Jeff Beck shoes on and bell bottoms for sure. Long hair picked out and plumed into a giant Afro. Shit, I *looked* like a guy who should be in the band.

And I knocked the tryout out of the park. I looked good, I played great, and I danced like a champ. I was the Muhammad Ali of saxophone players that night. Again, there was just this electricity flowing through that building. And BOMF was my way to jump in.

■ ■ ■

All of a sudden, I practically lived at the Record Plant. Otherwise, I would have been going back and forth to Brooklyn, and I just wanted to hang out at the studio *all the time*. And Roy Cicala, the studio owner and big-time producer who'd worked with everyone from the Four Seasons to John Lennon, let me stay. Roy was a big fan of BOMF, using the guys on this and that for various recording projects. So I put up a bed in the back room behind the rehearsal space, and Roy gave me a job cleaning up the place.

I was literally a janitor, cleaning up the garbage.

And I'd be downstairs, near Studios A and B, and I remember David Bowie and Mick Jagger being down on the ground floor near the payphones and one would be waiting for the other to get off so they could make a call.

And when you run into those guys, you gotta be chill. You don't want to be a drag. In other words, they appreciate that you don't stop and say, "Can I have your autograph?" You have some professional courtesy. So you give them a nod. They nod back to you. And it was like enough. Because in those situations, you gotta fight the impulse to want to say more.

But at the same time, if I'm cleaning out the trash and saying hello, I don't want to be known as just the trash guy. You want these guys to know, *Hey, I'm cool, too.* But they understood. For every instance I'd be slinging garbage, there were other times where I'd be in a room recording and I'd come out with a sax strapped around my neck. So, they got it. They knew we were all working the hustle, trying to be a part of the whole scene.

And that's the thing, there was music happening everywhere. Even at night, the place was going off. I remember one night I was sleeping in my little corner of the rehearsal room up on the tenth floor, and I heard bass and bass drums coming up from the stairwell. All of a sudden, there was like this *bumbaadumm, bumbaadumm.* The whole building was fucking quaking. And I remember wondering, *what the hell is that?* It was shaking the whole place and my teeth were rattling.

Turns out Jack Douglas, a monster producer/engineer who worked with everyone from the New York Dolls to the Who to John Lennon, was recording his second album with Aerosmith and had set up these massive speakers in the stairwell.[2] Probably Altec Lansings or maybe Sun cabinets or SBTs. And Jack was *pumping* the bass drum and the bass guitar through the speakers into the stairwell so he could record the massive sound. And this was like three o'clock in the morning! But at the same time, I probably wasn't too surprised. It was a creative joint and people were always getting sounds. And that's what Jack was doing at 3 AM:

---

2. Douglas got his foot in the door at the Record Plant the same way I did: working as a janitor. Soon he was at the recording desk as an engineer, contributing to projects by Miles Davis, the James Gang, Alice Cooper, Cheap Trick, Montrose, Rough Cutt, Artful Dodger, Moxy, Flipp, and Mountain.

getting those monster drum sounds for what would be Aerosmith's 1975 multi-platinum smash, *Toys in the Attic*.[3]

■ ■ ■

So, I'd been there a few months. Playing my horn and cleaning up garbage, bumping into big-time cats like Jagger and Bowie. Life was good.

But the guy I really wanted to meet was John Lennon.

A fellow Brooklynite, this cat Jimmy Iovine, was now engineering John Lennon's *Rock 'n' Roll* record with Roy Cicala as producer. Back in the day, Jimmy and I were in rival groups competing in the Battle of the Bands. My band always won, of course, but Jimmy was now making a name for himself in the studio world in a big way, coming off engineering Springsteen's *Born to Run*. So, the guy had juice.[4]

They were working out of Studio C, which was on the same floor as the rehearsal space. It was supposed to be just an overdub room, but more and more it got to be used as a main cutting room because of the privacy it afforded. I mean, there were people who wanted to book Studio C, rather than A or B. Because while both A and B had these massive drum rooms and live rooms, the bands

---

3. Rumor has it that Steven Tyler wrote out the original words to "Walk This Way" on the walls in the Record Plant stairwell, obviously the place to get stuff done for Aerosmith.

4. Jimmy is an industry titan. After his success with Bruce and Lennon, he went on to work with Patti Smith, Tom Petty and the Heartbreakers, U2, Stevie Nicks, Dire Straits, and the Pretenders. After forming Interscope Records, he teamed up with Dr. Dre to co-found Beats, which was later acquired by Apple, where Jimmy helped in the creation of Apple Music. Not bad for a kid from the old neighborhood.

were in a fishbowl. You were downstairs and everybody saw what you were doing.

And word was Lennon would come in up the back elevator, do his work in Studio C, and sneak out.

But then I ended up going into Studio C one day because Roy called me in for something. And fortunately I wasn't carrying or emptying garbage pails, because there he was, sitting at the console next to Roy. *John Lennon.* One of those mystery men on the back of that first Beatles record my Aunt Iris had bought me all those years before. The man who, more than any other, made me want to be a rock 'n' roller.

My head was spinning while Roy or Jimmy provided introductions, saying, "Oh yeah, it's Mark Rivera, he's with BOMF." By that time, John already knew of the band because a couple of the guys had already done handclaps and sang background parts on *Walls and Bridges.*

And he's in the middle of his session. So, there's only a simple, "Hi, nice to meet you."

And it's like, *what portal did I just walk into?* Not only am I in the same studio as John Lennon, but I remember they were talking about his vocals. And everyone knew that when he was with the Beatles, John would always tell producer George Martin to put his vocals more toward the back of the track. He was always sensitive about his tone, which he thought was too harsh or something. And now I'm in this studio, and they're listening back to vocals—and they sound fucking amazing—and John keeps pulling down the fader on his vocal, saying, "It's too much!"

It was like when I saw *The Wizard of Oz* as a kid. Or when Tinkerbell touched the peacock with her wand, and it all went to color. *Whoa!* That's the difference between this moment and any of the studios or rehearsal rooms I'd ever been in. Because this one had John Lennon. The man put color in my rock 'n' roll world.

So, I was kind of speechless. Which was good because, again, when you don't want to say stuff that's stupid, you should try not to speak.

I was only in the room for a few minutes. But here's the thing. If you are fortunate enough to be in the room at all, sometimes that's enough. Especially in an environment like the Record Plant where you could be a king, like a Lennon or a Bowie or a Jagger, or just a guy who's in charge of garbage bags once in a while. Everyone respected each other. Because you're all musicians, all members of a community, and the more that you play by the unwritten rule of *be cool and play your shit*, the more you might get pulled into something awesome.

That understanding and patience is huge for the sideman or anyone who wants to get into the music business. How you meet people is *everything*. Look, if I tell you, "Go into that room over there, and when you open the door, John Lennon's gonna be on the other side," how are you gonna react?

My advice? *Say as little as possible.* It's like my dad always used to tell us kids, "You have two ears and one mouth. Listen twice as much as you speak." And in the rock 'n' roll business, a good rule of thumb when you're the new guy is don't say too much. Don't step on your dick.

And that's the other thing—there are certain people who you can trust to be cool. Others, not so much. It doesn't make them bad people. I would never want to connect them with someone famous. They'd be stepping on their dick right and left.

So, I guess Roy and Jimmy knew I could hang. Otherwise, they wouldn't have let me in the building, much less the room, with John Lennon. It's pretty simple—you have to have a certain level of trust.

And that was HUGE because producers like Roy are matchmakers. They're always cognizant of who's being introduced to whom. And more than likely, Roy was calling me into that room for the specific reason of meeting John, to see how I'd handle it.

It wasn't like, "Hey, now you're John's best friend."

It was like, "You just met him. You've broken the ice."

That's the way things work, because soon after that, I was pulled further into John's sphere. *Much further.* At first it was the whole BOMF band with the televised *Salute to Sir Lew* and the bitchin' jumpsuits. Yeah, we played to track, but we added a couple of horn parts to "Imagine." So here I am now, recording new horns on "Imagine," one of my favorite songs of all time, and then I'm up on stage with John. That's a big-time gig.

And then, a few weeks later, John and Roy let me in a bit more. I remember Roy came up to me at the studio and saying, "So hey, by the way, John's producing Gary US Bonds. He needs a sax." So, I got to play on one or two sessions with Gary US Bonds, a rhythm and blues guy who'd had some big hits in the sixties, like "Quarter to Three" and "School Is Out," and had actually headlined *above* the Beatles on a European tour in 1963. So I was in the studio playing sax, and John is the producer, my friend Jimmy Iovine is the engineer, and I'm like, *holy shit,* my feet aren't touching the ground.

■ ■ ■

My time with John was short-lived—as quick as he showed himself, the mystery man disappeared again. He wouldn't return to the Record Plant for four years, when he would record his next and final album, *Double Fantasy.*[5]

---

5. John was at the studio and working on the song "Walking on Thin Ice" on December 8, 1980. He was shot and killed later that evening.

But I spent two years living out of that BOMF room. I just bounced around that whole time. A man without a country. I mean, I didn't even have a license. Still, I got around.

We had a BOMF truck, an old US mail truck that we bought for like two hundred bucks. It had right-hand steering—even more of a challenge for my unlicensed self. Still, I drove that thing up and down the city. I had some set of balls, boy. I remember driving the freaking thing at two-thirty in the morning, through the Brooklyn–Battery Tunnel, stoned out of my mind—high and wired up—and every time I'd pass a cop, my heart was in my throat. So, I'd be very conscientious not to drive over the speed limit. Still, it was stupid.

There'd be the gig, we'd load back up, have a few more drinks, a few more hits, then head out, and I'd eventually drive myself back to the Record Plant or home. And there'd be this ragged-out mailman truck with all of the gear in it parked on the street in Brooklyn in front of my parents' house. And there's their son without a license and, "Oh, gee, how did the truck get here?" It was obvious but my parents never said anything.

Sometimes we used to go to this place called Old Dutch, a dive diner in Brooklyn that was open twenty-four hours. At the end of a gig, we'd have a couple of drinks, smoke a couple bones, and we'd be hungry. So we'd go to Old Dutch for bacon cheeseburgers at two in the morning.

We'd go there like every other weekend and enjoy these bacon cheeseburgers—"Oh, this is great, this is great"—and the next time we'd go it would be closed by the Department of Health. So we'd go back a week or two later, and it'd be reopened and we'd have our bacon cheeseburgers: "Oh, this is great, this is great."

And Saturday nights we'd play Valentino's or Broadway Charlie's. Broadway Charlie's was our home. We played there three to five times a month. Sometimes Friday–Saturday back to back. It was on Thirteenth Street and Broadway and was a total shithole. But we had that place packed every time.

I remember when my girlfriend at the time, Dorothy, came to the club to see the band. She was with a couple of friends. And the barmaid was a tough girl. I can't remember her name, but she was all inked up. Anyway, she was waiting on Dorothy and the other girls, and there was an ashtray on the table, overflowing with cigarette butts and ash. So, Dorothy and one of her girlfriends said, "Would you mind cleaning this?" and the barmaid picked up the ashtray and threw it on the floor, right on Dorothy's shoe. That's the kind of place it was: just throw the shit on the floor and order a fucking drink already.

And we'd play our music, loud as shit.

So, it was just all a good time. I wasn't paying rent anywhere—I was living at home when I wasn't crashing in the BOMF room back at the Record Plant. Living like a vagabond.

Here, there, and everywhere.

(Credit © Allan Jannenbaum)

Masking up: With John Lennon and BOMF for the BBC's
A Salute to Sir Lew Grade. Waldorf Astoria Hotel,
NYC, April 18, 1975. (Credit © Allan Jannenbaum)

Still fits! Brewster, NY, 2022. (Credit: Rivera Family Collection)

14

VIBE

Brewster, New York, 2020

I had a gig this weekend. Well, sorta. There wasn't a live audience, but we were playing for cameras onstage at the Count Basie Theater. It's a fabulous venue, and the livestream went out to anyone watching from home.

The singer is a Frank Sinatra kind of guy, and he's armed with a five-piece band that's legit. Piano, drums, bass, and a couple horns. We did six Sinatra tunes and four Billy Joel tunes. Usually I do these gigs, and they're very simple. I go up and play five songs. He pays me $1,500 cash, and I go home. But this one was for charity. So, it was a worthwhile event, and it was nice just to be playing with the group.

But I've done these video performances a handful of times over these past few months, and I'm over it. You're playing, trying to get into it, but your heart is screaming to *bring back the crowd*. It's kind of like going on a date with someone you're not that into—like a mercy date. I even know she's not that into it, but I'm doing it because my mother said I had to.

And what was freaky about this gig was we weren't even facing the right direction. The cameras were at the back of the stage, so we had to turn the band around and play with the empty seats behind us. And during the set, every time the drummer or the bass player would do something groovy, I'd look back to say something like, "Yeah, cool," and I'd see that empty hall behind him and think, *what the fuck?* After fifty years of being in this business, I can't wrap my head around the emptiness.

And the Count Basie Theater is a classic place for people to watch a show. It's in Red Bank, New Jersey. We played there with Ringo; it's that kind of a venue where people want to play.

■ ■ ■

I remember I was playing the Count Basie Theater around 2005, and I ran into the one-of-a-kind Darlene Love (Sam Cooke, Elvis Presley, the Beach Boys) backstage. I first played with Darlene in 1982 in this little hole in the wall. She had been treated unfairly by the industry and hadn't played in about a decade before that.[1]

She has such a warm, kind spirit. Darlene said to me, "How are you, darling? It's so good to see you again after all this time."

And we're talking about family and sharing old stories, and I said, "Darlene, do you remember the first gig we did together, and the trumpet player fell over?"

"Honey, do I remember it?" she replied. "I still have a video of that man falling out!"

What happened was, while I was on break between Billy's shows for *The Nylon Curtain* and Simon & Garfunkel's tours, my

---

1. If you haven't seen the Academy Award–winning documentary *Twenty Feet from Stardom*, you should. Darlene, who is featured in the film, was an unsung hero singing on a lot of producer Phil Spector's songs in the 1960s. She ultimately sued Spector for unpaid fees/royalties and won!

friend Steven Van Zandt from the E Street Band asked me to put together a band for Darlene, who'd all but hung up music at the time. It was a crazy gig because nobody really knew her and we're playing this little shithole. I mean, I probably got paid like $300 to do the gig. But Darlene was amazing and won the band and the crowd over instantly. She was so super soulful.

But at the end of the set, she had this big singing crescendo, and the horns were blaring. My buddy Larry Etkin was on the trumpet and held this magnificent high note for so long that he actually hyperventilated and fell, knocking over three music stands. He was fine, but the audience was in shock, and it was a hell of the way to close the set.

Anyway, it was lovely to run into Darlene after twenty-some years and see her doing so well. She deserves everything she's received.

So now I'm back at that same theater, the Count Basie, for this video gig. There's nobody backstage to catch up with. There's nobody in the audience. A total buzzkill.

And the strangest thing isn't the sight of an empty hall as much as *the sound* of an empty hall. Sure, you're used to an empty venue for soundchecks, but that's not a performance. And when the people come and fill a venue, the sound changes. Because an audience soaks up sound. Their bodies, their clothes. They are literally absorbing the sound waves. And the more people, the more absorption.

Take, for instance, Madison Square Garden. You play sound-check to this great empty hall and the sound is reverberating all over the place. It's all concrete and steel. A giant, open cavity. But then you have the show, and that cavity gets jam-packed with people. Again, people have mass. They take up space. Their physical presence matters, and suddenly this cold, sterile hall turns into the cathedral for music it is.

God, do I miss that crowd in the Garden. Between all of the bands, I've probably played something like three hundred shows there. And with Billy, we'd basically been doing a show there once a month for the past ten years. I can close my eyes and almost put myself back there. *Almost . . .*

We're getting ready to take the stage. It's sort of like a countdown to liftoff.

T minus sixty seconds . . .

I'm on the side of the stage, I got last-minute things going through my mind—it's not nerves, but if I'm a boxer, I would imagine getting punches thrown at me, or a baseball player getting ready to go into the batter's box. Those pre-game thoughts are in your head. The PA music is still going on, the lights are on, you look around at the people—like, *they* weren't all here before! And at the Garden, it's always packed up to the top, top row.

T minus thirty seconds . . .

The lights go out and the crowd goes nuts. And now I'm walking up on a dark stage and there's this roar. Twenty thousand people, on their feet, sensing what's about to happen.

Five, four, three, two, one:

As soon as the light hits Billy and he starts playing piano, the crowd gets even louder. They've been waiting for this. I've been waiting for this, because even though I've done it a gazillion times, it just never gets old.

We often start shows with "Miami 2017," which Billy plays alone. But when the band starts up, that's when you notice the difference from soundcheck. It's the same onstage sound, but what you're getting out of your house speakers is different. You saw the people before the lights went out, then you heard the people. But now, you feel the people in the room. They're part of the acoustic space. Again, mass. That low frequency is going out and it's not coming back, because you know what the band is putting out there is being absorbed.

Ahhhh . . . people are here!

BOMF eventually dispersed. It lost its identity, and everyone went their separate ways. It happens.

It's the perfect example of a fun band that loses its vibe. I mean, we play together, everyone's having a great time. We invest in the mail truck, and it's all good stuff. But then something happens . . . and that something for BOMF was Lori Burton, Roy Cicala's wife.

Lori was a songwriter who glommed on to the band and pretty much took all the fun out of it. To be fair, she didn't stick her nose in as much as Roy said, "Hey, by the way, my wife wants to be in the band" or "She wants to sing some songs."

And soon that became "Lori wants to record one song," which became "She'd like to record two songs," to "Let her do a couple of those songs with you live," to "Maybe you guys can give Lori a whole set."

So, she winds up taking over a little bit more, then a little bit more. And some guys are okay with it because, *Hey look, if we give up a certain part of our set, maybe this leads to a good thing and we're all happy.*

But it doesn't really ever go there, does it? And the only thing it's doing is driving us fucking crazy. I mean, I was willing to play for little dough at a shithole, but there's got to be a good vibe happening.

And it wasn't anything overt. It's always just personality things. I mean, you spend a lot of time with people when you're in a band. It sounds petty, but what annoyed me most was her commentary on everyone's personal habits. Like, before or after shows I'd always have a burger and a malted, like really not a healthy thing. And she'd sit there next to me or simply be around saying,

"Oh, you and those burgers and malts—I can't deal with you. I can't deal with it."

And I always felt like saying, "I'm not asking you to deal with anything."

And we weren't the only ones having trouble with Lori's shit. Roy, her husband, became upset with Lori, too. *Depressed* is probably more the right word. I don't know if he was on medication. He probably was. But this one time she must have said something hot to him between sets, because he took out a gun on Broadway and fired it straight up in the air.

Piece in the air. *BOOM! BOOM! BOOM!*

I'm not even sure why he was packing, but he was, and I was like, *Whoa, this is getting a bit tricky here.*

Maybe it was a jealousy thing, or she was flirting too much with guys in the band or in the crowd, but her night on stage was her big night out. She would get dressed to the nines. I tried to stay out of it. But it was clear Roy had realized his brilliant idea to give his wife a band had come back to bite him in the ass.

Soon thereafter, we were all sort of like, "Well, this ain't fucking worth it."

■ ■ ■

It was around this time when BOMF disintegrated that I got involved with the band Tycoon. Norman Mershon, the lead singer, heard me play with BOMF. He was a carpenter at the Record Plant. He told me, "I have a band and we're doing a demo. Would you consider playing sax on two songs?"

So, I wound up joining the band. Jack Douglas, that same guy who was recording all the Aerosmith tracks, was recording our demos. *Holy shit.*

We did the recording and auditioned for three different record companies: one was Atlantic, one was I think maybe Mercury or whatever their subsidiary was then, and the other one was Arista, which was Clive Davis's new record company. They all loved the band, the songs, and whatever the other labels' numbers were— $180,000, $200,000—Clive said, "I'll give you $250,000." He gave us significantly more money than the other two.

Plus, it was Clive Davis. This is the man who'd signed the likes of Janis Joplin, Santana, Barry Manilow, Pink Floyd, Aerosmith, Billy Joel, and like a billion others. He could, obviously, make things happen.

Clive did have one stipulation: he didn't want to use Jack Douglas as the producer. But we're like, *No, Jack is our producer . . . he did this, he did that.*

And Clive said, "If you want to use Jack, go with Atlantic or the other company. I want you to use this new producer."

One of us said, "Who's that?"

Clive replied, "Mutt Lange."

We were all like, *What the fuck is a Mutt Lange?*

Of course, Mutt would go on to be a titan in the music world, producing and songwriting with everyone from AC/DC to Foreigner to Def Leppard, but at that time no one knew about him. So, we said okay to Clive and flew out to London to record the album with Mutt.

I hate to say it, but even playing with John Lennon was eclipsed by this. As much as playing with John was great, I wasn't participating much. Instead it was overdubbings, miming, one or two tracks we played over a live version of "Imagine." It was great, but playing with Tycoon was in a different league because I was now feeling like *I'm in a band*!

I'm twenty-five years old, and of course, as with Eclipse, I'm thinking, *Oh, I've totally made it. I'M GONNA BE A ROCK STAR!* I've signed with Arista Records, and now we're in London recording an album with this new producer that Clive Davis himself appointed. And the truth was that we needed all the help we could get. Our drummer was really not great. We had some great songs, but we needed direction. We needed those big vocal ideas. And we didn't have enough songs when we started out. So, two of the songs came along while we were there with Mutt.

Mutt was just *in it*. Very hands on. He'd pick up a bass. He'd pick up a guitar. He'd sing a vocal line. And Mutt and I definitely connected. We formed an instant friendship. Because for Mutt, *everything* was about the vibe. He'd always say, "It's gotta have the vibe. It's gotta have the vibe." He's not like a trippy guy, but he's got this way about him. It's a spirit.

And Mutt would say, "Markus"—which is what Mutt always called me—"you have the vibe for this, you got the vibe for that." And I was all over that record. Saxophone, percussion, backgrounds. He made me feel like a Swiss Army knife, relying on my musical abilities, but more importantly, my ability to get hip to the vibe.

At one point, he even talked to the band and said, "Mark has gotta sing a couple of the songs."

And Norman Mershon, the lead singer, said, "Okay, they're not really my type of songs anyway."

So, we cut two songs with me on vocals, and they're two of my favorite songs on the record.

■ ■ ■

Ultimately, not even Mutt Lange could bring Tycoon to stardom. I mean, we hadn't even left the studio and we'd already decided to fire the drummer. This gives you an idea of how unsettled things were. Then we came back to the States, getting promotional pictures with the new drummer, and the guitar player said, "I don't think I want to be in a touring band. I want to stay home and do more sessions and be a session musician."

Now two of the guys are gone. And it goes to shit to shit to shit.

I remember we had a practice space on Eighth Avenue and Thirty-Eighth Street. It's the Music Building, which is now world renowned. It's fourteen stories, about six rehearsal rooms per floor. It's like total cacophony unless you spend a lot of money to sound-proof it. But we had a room and we thought we could actually be recording, which is another expense. And I was thinking, *what are we doing here?*

By that time, the band was on to our third guitarist and third drummer. The record had flopped, and Clive Davis had all but forgotten us. It was just not happening.

I was already gigging with other bands. It was what I did. It was the way of keeping my craft *and* my sanity. Because I could be down in the dumps about not making it, but really, I just wanted to keep playing. I wanted to keep getting back up on stage, and Tycoon never really gigged. We recorded and played a couple shows, opening for Heart and the Little River Band. It wasn't performance driven, and I loved to perform. Recording and spending money to *maybe* make it? *Fuck that.*

Let's get people dancing. Let's get people grooving. Let's get *in the vibe.*

■ ■ ■

When you're growing as a musician, you want to keep going up the ladder, not stand in one place. You want to expand your horizons. And after climbing the BOMF and Tycoon rungs, I climbed another step and started to play with the people at the really elite New York clubs: Trax, Mikell's, JP's, Home, Eric's, and Max's Kansas City.

Especially Trax and JP's. The owner of those two clubs, this guy Jimmy Pullis, had an eye for talent and booked semi-obscure artists, like Warren Zevon, who would later find stardom. And everyone liked to hang there. It was sort of like the Record Plant in that musicians of all stripes, including celebrities—say, a Paul Simon or Carole King—might find themselves at JP's or Trax at some point in the evening.[2]

I remember the first time I played JP's. I got a call from this guy Jimmy Frank, who said, "Hey man, I got your name from so-and-so, and I'm just new in town from Los Angeles. I'm auditioning for a gig at JP's this afternoon."

I said, "Oh, cool."

He goes, "Can you bring your horn?"

Now, I don't know this guy from Adam, but he's calling me up and asking if I want to do a gig. And you can't climb the ladder of success by saying no. The phone rings and you have to say, "Sure, man!"

So I headed down to 1971 First Avenue, near Seventy-Sixth Street, for the tryout. And I walk into the place and there's a guy setting up a keyboard.

I say, "Hi, I'm Mark. Are you Jimmy?"

And the guy looks at me like I'm some asshole and goes, *"Am I Jimmy?* You mean you don't even know the guy you're auditioning with?"

So, obviously, the guy wasn't Jimmy. He was the house sound guy, and he just put on this whole attitude of, *Oh, this is gonna suck,* which wasn't the way I wanted to start things off.

Then the real Jimmy Frank walks in. We say hello and he sits at the piano and starts playing. Just the two of us for about twenty minutes. No warmup or "hey, these are the chords." And the

---

2. Of Trax and JP's, the *New York Times* reported, "Together they are to the world of rock-and-roll what Elaine's is to the celebrity-literature crowd." Elaine's, of course, was also located on the Upper East Side, and frequented by such notable writers as Norman Mailer, Gay Talese, Woody Allen, and Joseph Heller. (John Rockwell, "The Pop Life: Trax and JP's Cater to Trade," *New York Times,* March 24, 1978.)

sound guy who gave me the stink eye earlier books us a spot for that fucking night. We were that good.

Jimmy and I put a band together called Trouble, and the sound guy, whose name was Teddy Leonard, booked us multiple days each week for the next three years. It was a sick band. We had Jimmy Bralower (Madonna, Steve Winwood, Peter Gabriel) on drums; my friend Rick Pasquale, whom I'd known since I was seventeen, on bass; and this guy Jimmy Ryan on lead guitar. Jimmy Ryan was Carly Simon's guitarist, recording the solo on "You're So Vain" in 1972. So, I was meeting and playing with really accomplished musicians.

Trax was the same deal. Talk about a select group of players. I mean, there was Yogi Horton, the greatest drummer that I'd ever played with. He was the first real R&B drummer who had it, and he worked with everyone. I mean Aretha, Diana Ross, the Spinners . . . *everyone.*

And Yogi was *way* down in the lint. Everything he did was just cool. He played cool, looked cool, talked cool. I remember one rehearsal was in the dead of summer. We're talking dog days. And I was wearing these Everlast boxing shorts, like bright red, on my skinny-ass legs with Converse sneakers and a white wife-beater shirt. And Yogi takes one look at me and goes, "Yo, look at my boy, Sugar Rico," after the superstar boxer Sugar Ray Leonard. And everyone in the band fucking rolled, laughing their asses off. And of course, the name stuck. Just like his sick backbeats, when Yogi said something, it made an impression on everyone. And I've been "Sugar Rico," or "Sug" or "Ric," to all my dear friends ever since.

And on the same bandstand at Trax was an amazing female keyboard player/singer/songwriter, Bette Sussman. She had tremendous talent and would go on to be Whitney Houston's musical director. (We all knew Whitney and her sister, Sissy Houston, from Mikell's, up on Ninety-Seventh Street.)

Finally, there was Jimmy Rippetoe, a.k.a. Jimmy Rip. He was our guitarist and went on to play with Mick Jagger and be his musical director.

So, this rhythm section—Yogi, Bette, Jimmy, and myself—was the real deal. The other pieces, like the bass player, would rotate, but the four of us were essentially the house band for any solo artist looking to make a splash. I don't know if any of these artists got a career of their own, but we sure as hell did. And every night we had gigs—an 8 PM show at Trax, which is on Seventy-Second Street off Broadway, then a cab ride over to Second Avenue and Sixty-Fourth Street for a 10 PM show at JP's, and back to Trax for a midnight show. And $100 each set meant $300 a night. Enough to get us high, have a good time, and stay up until 5 AM.

Jimmy Pullis, the owner of both clubs, loved us. I remember one night we wrapped early and everyone went home. And there was a big event at Madison Square Garden that night, part of the "No Nukes" concert series in 1979. It was a huge deal—James Taylor, Russ Kunkel, Joni Mitchell, Bonnie Raitt. Anyway, the concert wrapped, and they all headed to Trax. So Jimmy Pullis called us up, saying, "You got to come back to Trax! These big cats are coming out!" Jimmy knew everyone in the city who was worth a damn behind an instrument. But he was calling us because he wasn't about to screw around.

Like Mutt Lange, Jimmy wanted the best of the best—the people he considered not only proficient but who also brought *the vibe*: that enthusiasm for what others are doing and a sincere willingness to give them your energy and attention. Why would a sideman do anything less?

15

MR. LORD

Brewster, New York, 2020

I caught up with my old friend Doane Perry yesterday. He's been a drummer on big stages for like four decades, manning the throne with acts like Dragon, Jethro Tull, Lou Reed, Ian Anderson, and Martin Barre.

Like me, Doane was with a bunch of smaller bands in New York City in the '70s, and it's gotta be forty-five years since Doane and I played together, a weekly gig at a place on Greene Street in Greenwich Village. But musicians share a bond with the guys they came up with. It's sort of like the military—you remember and love the people who were with you in the trenches. Because every night was a fight to keep your spot on the line. You had to keep your chops up and your attitude positive. You had to say yes to everything and then figure out how the hell to get it done and get it done well, because lots of musicians would have given their eyeteeth to have been in that NYC scene, and if you couldn't step up, someone else would and the chance would blow right by you.

Anyway, Doane now lives out in California, so we only talk a few times a year, but when we do, the conversation just flows and we talk about everything. At some point during yesterday's chat we swapped stories about the Fillmore East. Doane grew up on the East Side in the Village, and like any city kid who was into rock 'n' roll in the late '60s/early '70s, the Fillmore East was that place you went to see your favorite bands.

So, Doane tells me this great story about seeing the band Jethro Tull at the Fillmore in 1970. He was fourteen at the time and idolized the band's drummer, Clive Bunker, and somehow managed to get inside for the band's soundcheck. After it was over, he wrote a note to Bunker, saying how much he would like to meet the band, and gave the note to the security guard. Long story short, security led Doane upstairs into the dressing room at the Fillmore East, where he got to meet the whole band, including their iconic front man, Ian Anderson, who said, "So who's this little pusher here?" They were all impressed that this young kid had the balls to make his way backstage.

Fast-forward a decade later and Jethro Tull is looking for a new drummer. And who do they pick? Doane Perry. That same fourteen-year-old kid who needled his way into meeting the band at the Fillmore East, who'd been pounding it out the previous five years in every NYC bar and club he could.

It's a great story, especially because Doane wound up playing the gig for nearly forty years.

So now it's my turn and I say, "Did I ever tell you about the time I met Jon Lord?"

And Doane starts laughing and says, "Tell me the story."

I went to see Deep Purple and Creedence Clearwater Revival in 1968 at the Fillmore East. Deep Purple was the opening act. Of course, they blew my mind, especially Jon Lord, who was the band's keyboardist and responsible for the organ on the band's hit song "Hush," which I considered the best fucking organ solo in all of rock.

So now we're between acts, and I'm sneaking down closer to the stage because my seat sucked, and I find something like in the eighteenth row. A few minutes later, this guy sits next to me and it's none other than Jon Lord. I guess he wanted to catch the CCR show from the seats. So now I'm freaking out because this is one of my biggest influences and I'm thinking, "Should I say anything to him?" Because I'm just this skinny fifteen-year-old kid, and he's got this huge moustache and this big Jesus Christ-long red hair. Like super fucking cool. But I get up the nerve and say, "Uh, Mister Lord?"

And he looks over at me and smiles. "Please, call me Jon."

And now I suddenly couldn't shut up. I said, "You were amazing up there . . . you blew the whole crowd away . . . the solo on 'Hush' is the greatest thing I've ever heard. . ." On and on I went–blah blah blah blah–stumbling over my words.

But he was very gracious and just said, "Thank you, man. Thank you."

You could tell he liked me because I was so enthusiastic, but he also was kind of like, "Okay, kid, it's time to stop talking now." So, I finally stepped on my tongue and Creedence came on. A few songs into the set and Jon Lord was gone, probably backstage or wherever.

So, I tell Doane all of this over the phone, and he's laughing and says it's a great story.

"But it's not over," I say. Like his Jethro Tull story, there's another chapter.

Because almost forty years later in 2007, I was called to be the musical director for Jim Capaldi's tribute in London. The legendary drummer and co-writer for Traffic had died two years earlier from cancer, and his wife organized a huge benefit concert that included Stevie Winwood, Pete Townshend, Joe Walsh, Paul Weller, Yusuf Islam (formerly known as Cat Stevens), Gary Moore, and Bill Wyman.

So, I'm in London, rehearsing with the band, which featured another who's-who list of names, like drummers Andy Newmark (Sly and the Family Stone, Pink Floyd) and Simon Kirke (Free, Bad Company), percussionist Ray Cooper (Elton John, Paul McCartney), Paul "Wix" Wickens (Paul McCartney, Elton John), and last but certainly not least, Deep Purple's organ maestro, Jon Lord. So, it's a killer band and we're doing Traffic songs and I'm doing flute, sax, and also doing the singing duties until the headliners arrive the day before the show. And meanwhile, I'm like holding a boner down the whole time because I'm playing with these cats and getting to sing all of these incredible tunes.

At the end of the second day of rehearsals, I say to Jon, "You have to indulge me."

He says, "What is it?"

I said, "I would give my eyeteeth to sing 'Hush.'"

And everyone in the band is like, "Yeah, 'Hush!'"

So, we play "Hush." And I can't believe it. "Holy shit! I'm singing 'Hush' with Jon Lord." And at the end of the whole thing, I said, "I gotta tell you a quick story."

He said, "What's that?"

I said, "Do you remember years ago when Deep Purple opened up for Creedence Clearwater at the Fillmore East, and after you played, you came out and sat in the audience."

And Jon looked at me, and I swear to God, without me saying another word, he smiled and goes, "You were that kid!"

And I was like, "Yes!" I couldn't believe he remembered that, and he grabbed me in this big hug, and we started laughing and I got tears in my eyes. It was like, *fuck!* That was forty years earlier!

After that we had this amazingly wonderful relationship. He was supposed to only play organ on one or two things. But he played organ on everything except when Stevie Winwood played organ. It was unbelievable.

So now I'm on the phone outside next to the pool, telling my good friend this story. And he's laughing and then Sandra comes out and says, "Anytime now . . ." because I'd been on the phone for over an hour and we're now running late to get somewhere.

And I think I said, "Oh, shit," so Doane and I had to end the conversation. But it was great to catch up and reminisce. Two old vets from the NYC music scene who went on to have careers in this crazy business. It makes me realize that I am this culmination of every single encounter I've had in my life. And how chance has smiled on me a number of times. Fortunately, when chance came knocking on the door, I wasn't busy doing something else. I just said yes and opened the door.

16

MUTT'S ON THE PHONE

■ **New York City, 1980**

It started out like any other night. I played at Trax until about 10:30 PM, took a cab because I had two saxophones, and carried them up the six flights of stairs to my apartment. Then the phone rang.

"Hello, Markus. It's Mutt."

"Hi Mutt, great to hear from you . . ."

"I'm wondering if you could come down to Electric Ladyland Studios."

"Sure, when?" I asked.

"Right now."

I was like, "Oh man, I'm shagged. I've just been playing and came up six flights of stairs."

"Well, I'm recording Foreigner's new record," Mutt explained. "And they need a saxophone bit."

Wait . . . what?

It's hard to overstate how big of a band Foreigner was during that time. Their initial albums, *Foreigner* and then *Double Vision*, went multi-platinum and helped rock 'n' roll reclaim the Top 40 airwaves and send disco packing. Even their latest, *Head Games*, released in 1979 and underwhelming by the band's superstar standards, climbed to #5 on the *Billboard* 200 chart, receiving platinum certification only four months after it hit the stores. And now it seemed the band was teaming up with my good friend Mutt, who himself was fresh off blockbuster success with AC/DC's *Back in Black*.

Needless to say, I was downstairs and in a cab on my way to the studio about three seconds after the phone hit the receiver.

■ ■ ■

Electric Ladyland is located in the Village where Eighth Street becomes St. Mark's Place and, in the music world of the late 1970s and early '80s, was the place of all places to be. Jimi Hendrix had the studio built and was instrumental in its design. Always painstaking, studio design is near impossible when you're trying to isolate sound amid the cacophony of the big city, and the project ran into its first of many problems when a canal that crossed beneath Eighth Street flooded the basement after engineers tried to install the acoustically isolated subfloor. For years, Hendrix kept getting screwed on his passion project, and he never got to enjoy the fruits of his labor, dying less than a month after Electric Ladyland was finally complete.

So now I was at the studio Jimi had built with one of the biggest bands on the planet waiting inside for me. I rang the bell and there's a camera.

"Who's that?" a woman asked over the intercom.

"Uh, Mark Rivera," I said. "I'm here to see Mutt Lange."

The door buzzed and I headed down a flight of stairs, and they're dark purple with these murals of a bunch of naked ladies on the walls. It's almost like going deeper and deeper into an acid trip, which I'm sure was Hendrix's desired effect. And I kept asking myself, *Is this really happening?* I'd had a few drinks at the club and probably a joint after the gig, but by now I was a hundred percent sober. But it was all just so surreal—I mean I'd been sweating it out on the club stage only an hour before, playing for like fifty bucks or whatever. And now I'm carrying my tenor saxophone, walking into rock 'n' roll's inner sanctum in the middle of the night about to do a session with Foreigner. It was bizarre, and even the naked ladies on the walls with their coy expressions seemed to be asking what the hell I was doing here and if I was worthy of the gig.

Well, I thought as I approached the main studio, *I guess we're about to find out.*

■ ■ ■

Mutt Lange, Mick Jones, and Lou Gramm were in the studio's common room, playing foosball. The ball was banging around, and somebody scored because then they were screaming and hooting and hollering. Walking into the room, I noticed the bottles of vodka and the lines of coke on the counter. These guys had been here a while. Mick had a drink and Lou had a bottle. Mutt, who didn't drink or do drugs, was having club soda or tea.

And Mutt sees me and gives me this amazing hug, showing nothing but love. He then introduces me to Mick, the Englishman, who goes, "Oh yes, I've heard quite a bit about you." And it's a weird thing when a person like Mick Jones says that because it's implied that you have a lot to prove before he accepts whatever it is he's heard. He's very reserved, whereas Lou Gramm, an American from Rochester, New York, was all, "Hey, man, nice to meet you!" They couldn't have been more different.

Then Mutt said, "Let's play Markus the track." We went into the control room, and I remember these massive speakers and Mutt saying, "Okay, Markus. This is a song called 'Urgent,'" and he pressed Play, and right from the opening measures I was thinking the sound was fucking amazing. Apparently, Mutt had taken to a riff that Mick had recorded on a demo and now they'd constructed a whole song around it. It was an irresistible groove, layered in multiple bass lines, rhythm guitars, and drums to create this sound and energy that was at once very Foreigner but also unlike anything I'd ever heard. And I remember the hair on the back of my neck standing up because I had no doubt that the song was a hit. You just knew it in those opening measures, even before Lou's voice came in, which when it did was like a hand slipping into a glove. The man simply had one of the best voices ever to be recorded. And on this song, it was pure magic. The whole thing was beautifully constructed, and again, completely groundbreaking.

And yet, here I was, being asked to somehow make the track even better.

■ ■ ■

It wasn't a huge part they needed from me. There was a spot for a big sax solo but Mick said, "We've already called Junior Walker to handle that." Junior Walker, Motown's right-hand sax man, was a beast on the instrument. I'd met him a few years prior and told him I was a huge fan. Then I said, "Hey man, what's the setup?" In other words, *what kind of mouthpiece and reed do you use?* It's not a strange question; players ask that of each other all the time. But when I asked Junior what his setup was, he covered his mouthpiece, saying, "Hey man, that's something everybody has to find for themselves."

So that was Junior Walker, and he was slated to do the solo, which was fine by me. Again, I was happy as a pig in shit simply to be in the room.

Then Mutt rewound the tape and said, "We need something coming out of the first and second chorus. Just a hook to tie it all together." It was the only instruction he gave me.

So now I'm in the live room, and it's sort of like you're in this fishbowl. There's only me inside the bowl, and I'm looking out to the control room, through the glass, and there's these superstars on the other side. Rock royalty. And you gotta realize, Mick and Lou are jacked up and so the A/C is on thirty degrees and I was thinking, *You could hang meat in this place.* But at least my reed was warmed up from playing earlier in the night, and it only took a minute to get things sounding right.

So, I've got the cans on, and Mutt is talking to me over the talkback mic. "Just do your thing, Markus. We'll run the track and get a vibe going," he says. What he means is he's gonna play the song from the top and I can just start playing to it so we can get the volume in my headphones right and the engineer can get his levels. Then, once everything is a go, they'll record some passes. How many passes? It could be a couple. It could be a hundred . . .

■ ■ ■

When you get a minute, go to iTunes or whatever and put on "Urgent" and TURN IT UP. Listen to those opening measures and pretend you're me in this moment. You gotta add something— but not too much. Something to complement the incredible drive that's already happening. *When exactly do you come in and what do you play?*

The first spot was only two measures, and the second was eight measures. Summed together, we're talking less than twenty seconds of the whole song. But trying to squeeze a worthwhile part in between other, established parts is tough, especially in a frenetic song like "Urgent" where shit is coming in and out all over the stereo field. It's like trying to parallel park a car on a busy street and there's no margin for error between the car in front and the car behind, and in the back of your mind, you're like, *I think it's okay, I hope it's okay. God, it better be okay.*

But here's the thing: from the time I'd met Mutt when I was playing with Tycoon up to the moment he'd called me up, I'd probably played a thousand gigs. For the past two years plus, I'd continued to play. Every night and with different acts. And whatever those acts needed, I brought to the table. So that competence was, in this moment with Foreigner, my ace in hole.

The song starts and suddenly my juices are flowing. This song, aptly named, just creates these urges inside your body, and like good sex, you can't help but want to get in there. So, I've got my sax to my lips and I'm totally grooving to the track. Again, I can't help it. It's like seeing a beautiful woman, and while at first you thought you could never have a shot—now, all of a sudden, you're swapping spit with her, and you're in it, and it's the greatest moment of your life. You're totally engrossed.

And yeah, I was still aware of the fishbowl and the tight sonic spaces, but all of that was on the periphery when we got to the end of the first chorus, the first spot, and I just played what I was feeling. We then cruised past the next verse, the next chorus, and again I played what was resonating in my bones. Sure, the level in the cans wasn't quite right, but that's actually better, because when it's not as loud as it needs to be, you play harder, with more of an edge. And this song definitely called for an edge.

We got to the end and I asked, "How does it sound?"

And Mutt had this big smile on his face and said, "It sounds great, man."

So, we get the levels adjusted and now Mick and Lou are telling me what they want. They'd sort of been hanging out in the corner when Mutt ran that first pass for levels, not really paying attention, but now they're coming at me with all of these ideas. So, I played maybe two or three takes of one idea. And then they had another idea, and we tried that one. And then they said, "Work on it for a while." So, I'm doing another take while they go outside for more vodka, more foosball. And that became the joke: *foosball, vodka, take. Foosball, vodka, take.* Over and over again. They'd crushed the bottle and probably played six games of foosball in the time I'm trying to get this fucking track done.

It's about 4:30 AM. I've been playing for like four hours and finally Mutt calls us all in and says, "I want you to hear something." Mutt presses the playback button and we listen to the whole song and it gets to my part and Mick and Lou freak out.

"That's perfect!" Mick shouts. "It's like this Morse code kind of spurt thing."

And Mutt smiles and says, "That was the first thing he played when he walked into the room."

Evidently, when we were just "getting sounds," Mutt could see that I was in the zone and hit the red button. He'd recorded the whole first pass, and it worked.

■ ■ ■

I'd obviously passed the audition with Foreigner, and I don't know if it was the following day or whatever but the next thing I knew, I was in the vocal booth helping them cut the background vocals. Mutt had said something like, "Oh, and by the way, Mark's a killer singer." And that's all it took.

On previous Foreigner records, Lou always sang the back-ups with this guy Ian Lloyd from the band Stories, but now it would include Mutt and myself.[1] The four of us were really strong together. "Jukebox Hero," "Waiting for a Girl Like You," "Night

---

1. Ian Lloyd was most famous for singing with the band Stories and their big hit "Brother Louie"—"Louie, Louie, Louie, Lou-eeeeee." Interestingly, it wasn't an original. A UK band called Hot Chocolate wrote and recorded it, rising to #7 in the UK. Six months later, Stories re-recorded and released it in the US and saw it go all the way to #1 on the *Billboard* Hot 100, selling over a million records.

Life" . . . those are some of the best backgrounds ever. And it wasn't just one song—I was on the entire album.

A few days later, Mutt goes, "He also plays keyboards and guitar." He was on his way out the door, heading for Australia to record the next AC/DC record and then another band out of England called Def Leppard.[2] And now Mick and Lou wanted me in the touring band! It was amazing how much Mutt had my back. It all happened so fast, and all from that one phone call from Mutt.

■ ■ ■

The album on which "Urgent" appeared, 4, was mammoth, going #1 on the charts and selling more than six million copies in the US alone. I remember between the recording and the tour starting, I was in San Francisco visiting my girlfriend. I'd borrowed a car and I was driving around town. It's a beautiful day. All of a sudden, I hear my voice on the radio, and then my saxophone. It was "Urgent" coming through! I had never heard myself on the radio before. Tycoon had some traction with the charts, but we never had a radio hit.

Soon, "Jukebox Hero" and "Waiting for a Girl Like You" were in regular rotation too. But I remember on that first day in San Francisco, pulling over and listening to the DJ: "This is the greatest thing Foreigner has ever put out. It is a groundbreaking record."

And all I kept thinking was, *Hey. That's me on that fucking record.*

Then we were on a world tour to match, playing to millions of fans. It was larger than anything I'd ever experienced in my life. Because now you're up on stage and you're playing "Hot Blooded"

---

2. The Def Leppard album was *High 'n' Dry*, his first effort with the band. Mutt would go on to produce their smashes, the iconic *Pyromania* and *Hysteria* albums, writing and cowriting most of the songs.

or "Double Vision" and the crowd reaction is INTENSE. It's forty, fifty, or sixty, eighty thousand people, larger than you ever thought it could be, and the roar of the crowd hits your whole body. People recognized the song, and the place would blow up. I'd never had that. Even forty years later, there's really no getting used to it, but as time goes on, you at least anticipate it. But those first times up on stage with Foreigner, it would hit you and the adrenaline coursing through your body would be insane. Like driving a car and accelerating to two hundred miles an hour and not stopping. You just keep going around the track.

It was all new. I mean, you're jumping from the club scene to suddenly playing on these big stages, and now you're doing your part, not only with other musicians, but in concert on a huge stage with hundreds of lights and big giant spotlights. And the monitors are now beneath the stage to make room for these giant ramps that move up and down the stages. And you suddenly have tons of space to move around. I mean, it's not like I had a wireless mic back then at Trax! But now I have one and I can do whatever I want. I see a girl over on the left I like, I'm gonna go over to her. Another one on my right, she's next. And when the moment comes for my solos, I'm gonna leap off those Marshall stacks, like five feet up in the air, and the crowd is gonna go ballistic.

17

THE HIGH LIFE

Sideman, front man . . . whatever man. There's a balancing act between all of us. *You know what I'm gonna play and I know what you're gonna play.* But to a point. Because there's also some wiggle room. Some room for expression. Some room for spontaneity. How much depends on the song, the crowd, what the boss is willing to allow. But that's the thing—I've always worked with people who understand that spontaneity is the life that keeps the party going. It keeps things interesting and each of the players on their toes.

As I've become older, I save more and more of life's spontaneity for the stage. I've got my routines at home and before shows and afterward, and I guess as the years have progressed, I've become more and more a creature of those habits. It happens. But when I was younger, especially in those early days with Foreigner, life on Planet Rock Star was just so new. On and off stage. And like a baby, I had to touch it, smell it, taste it. I'd see something and wonder, *Now, what's this?*

SIDEMAN

■ 1980-1982

We stayed in these five-star hotels all over the world, especially in Europe—Paris, London, Germany. And when we'd leave the hotel, we'd get onto a first-class flight. Now, as I'm leaving the hotel room one morning, I see a bottle of champagne. So, I stuck it in my knapsack, because *hey, a bottle of champagne. I'm taking it.*

This was before you had to worry about taking liquids on a plane. So, I get onto a first-class flight where they're serving enough champagne you could drown a horse in it, and I decide to carry my champagne because I might have it on the way to the next hotel. Then I just fell into taking the room champagne and minibar items at each stop.

Fast-forward to the end of the first tour. Lo and behold, they wanted to give me a $10K bonus. Bud Prager, Foreigner's manager, said to me, "Mark, the guys love having you and we want you on the next record. We want you in the band going forward. The band wants to give you a $10K bonus."

I'm like, *Far out!* I'm expecting a $10K check. But that's not what happened. The check I got was for like $5K. I'm like, "Oh . . . did you take out taxes or something?"

Bud says, "No, Mark, the champagne and other booze in the room is all minibar."

I got about $4K of minibar charges over the course of fourteen months. I swear, I had no idea. I literally thought, *Oh, it comes with the room.* No, it does not. And each bottle of champagne was probably $100 a pop.

I even said to Bud, "I swear I didn't know!" I'm throwing myself at the mercy of the court. You know, when some guy kills his own parents, but then says, "Please! I'm an orphan now!"

I'm like, "I drank all the champagne. Have mercy on me!"

Bud just had this laugh that said it all: *Welcome to the big time.*

It's ridiculous how uninformed I was. When you're on the road and on tour for over a year, it's very easy to lose track of your personal accounting. It's one stop to the next, lubricated by these bottles of champagne. It's all fun and games, but at the end, someone is calculating everything. Suddenly, the bill comes due, and it's like, *Hey guys, that was a great ride, but somebody's keeping track. There's a bottom line to this.*

Fortunately, I had a partner in crime and someone who could help show me the ropes. His name was Bobby Mayo. Bobby was the guitarist for Peter Frampton and the most amazing musician I'd ever met. He had perfect pitch, played the keyboards like Richard Tee (Aretha Franklin, Simon & Garfunkel, Quincy Jones), and played the guitar like Stevie Ray Vaughan. And Bobby could execute. No matter how big the stage or bright the lights, the guy could handle his end and more.

There's a great story about Bobby when he was with Frampton that my friend Mark Snyder told me. Frampton was getting ready to do this huge video production. So it's live cameras all over the place. And Peter's freaking out. There in this pre-production meeting, everybody's glued to Peter and his needs—"oh, yes Peter, yes Peter." Everyone except for Bobby, who's eating this big bowl of spaghetti. And Peter asks him how the fuck he can be eating anything right now and Bobby just shrugs his shoulders. It's like *Yeah, it's a five-pointer and you want me to play piano and guitar and sing . . . what's the big fucking deal?* Bobby was so cool and could obviously handle whatever the guys from Foreigner threw at him. Second guitar, keyboards, background vocals. There was no chair too big for Bobby Mayo.

But it's important to remember that Bobby Mayo and I were hired guns. Sidemen. The real members of the band were Mick, Lou, Dennis Elliott, and Rick Wills. Take a look at any promotional materials from that time, and it was just the four of them.

Maybe you'd catch a glimpse of Bobby and me faded out in the background like a couple of replaceable rockers. But they were the main guys, and you wouldn't forget it.

Take this, for instance. After a big show, we'd hop on this beast of a charter called a Viscount, a four-engine, turboprop plane that likely saw time during the Korean War. The beautiful thing of such a spacious, old plane is that it could fly on one prop if it had to, which makes it one of the safest things in the sky. So anyways, we're all changing out of our sweaty clothes, goofing off, drinking again. (You better believe that on a Foreigner flight, I'm not pulling out any stowaway champagne bottles, because I know the bar is stacked and we'll be getting high.) And Bud walks on with four paper bags, one for each of the guys. Now, even if the numbers were light and the band is doing something like $6 per head in merchandise, that's $240K in T-shirts and memorabilia for one of the "small" shows and double that when we're playing the larger venues. Sure, some of that is in credit cards, but plastic wasn't as in vogue then as it is now. So, 80 percent was in cash. Then you'd have to leave some cash on the books to use when buying the new merch. But still, I'd bet each one of these guys was walking with at least $20K a night in cash. Every fucking show.

I remember those little brown paper bags—like something you'd put potatoes in. How could anyone forget? Full of $20s, stocked full of money. That's how it was.

■ ■ ■

Mick had this incredible suite in our hotel in Nice.[1] It was like a three-bedroom, four-bathroom palatial thing with a seventeenth-century armoire and all these old paintings. He left a day early,

1. Matter of fact, this was the same hotel where I proposed to Sandra after knowing her for about two weeks. But that's a story for another time . . .

going back to London, because we had a couple days off before the Rome show and he was smitten with a girl named Ann.[2] Mick's room was where all the champagne, booze, and drugs were. So naturally, we took it upon ourselves to have a little suite party in Mick's absence.

And it was wild. It was me, Bobby Mayo, Peter Reilich, who was the second keyboardist, and a bunch of the other guys and some of their wives. We're smoking. We're drinking. There's blow. And then Alex King, the tour manager, walks in, and the party stops. *Record scratch.* He looks at me and Bobby, and I'm thinking we just got called to the principal's office, like something is wrong. He's a proper Englishman, and he says, "Now, Robert and Mark, would you two consider taking an earlier flight because two of the wives have been bumped off the plane?"

And we said, "Go to Rome early? Heck yeah."

So, because it was already 4 AM, why bother wasting time sleeping? So Bobby and I looped. They got us a flight at 8 AM, so we had to leave the hotel at 6:30, no big deal.

The rest of the band was going to show up on the later flight, which meant they'd get in around 1 PM, and Atlantic Records, who laid out the red carpet everywhere we went, had this mammoth luncheon set up for us. So, Bobby and I arrive about 10 AM, and a car takes us to the hotel. We've got some hours to kill, and Bobby spots this mopeds-for-rent stand. Sometimes he and I wouldn't even have to talk; we just knew what the other was thinking. It was like that onstage and it was like that right then because we were both thinking, *What better way to see Rome than by moped?*

Let me tell you, it's one of the greatest days of my life. I'm having a blast. I'd just met my future wife. I'm high on love, high

---

2. Ann would later become Mrs. Mick Jones. I remember Mick being so head over heels for Ann. He loved her so much.

on coke, high on booze, high on Rome, and we're tripping around, zipping through ancient Rome on shiny red Vespas.

Now it's about 1:15, 1:30, and the Atlantic Records person said to get back and clean up because there'd be this beautiful luncheon set up for us. So, we get there and I'm telling you, it was a banquet table about thirty feet long completely covered in a spread of food like nothing you've ever seen before—everything and anything you could possibly want to eat: magnificent foods, pastas, shrimp, lobster, steak, and it's only the two of us. And the guy from Atlantic says, "I don't know where they are—you eat."

You didn't have to tell us twice. Bobby and I ate like we were going to the electric chair. And then the guy said, "There's another dinner tonight at 8 PM. Shall I see you then?"

"Of course, sure!"

So, Bobby and I get back on the mopeds—just trip out, don't think about it. *There's the Colosseum, there's the Pantheon! How about the Trevi Fountain?*

But soon it's 7:30 at night, and we gotta clean up because our faces are full of soot from the day.

We finally get to this second Atlantic meal for us—and now, the whole band is there with their wives, and Bobby and I are like, "We had the greatest fucking day! You should've been here!"

We're going on and on—*We saw this! We saw that!*—about how, short of seeing the pope and wearing his hats, we had the greatest day ever. But these guys are pissed off. Bobby and I didn't know why. We're still basking in Rome's glory, but then this guy Troby Laidlaw, the assistant tour manager, pulls me aside and says, "Tone it down."

I go, "What the fuck?"

As it turns out, Peter Reilich, the other keyboard player, took something from the hotel that he shouldn't have. Peter was a nice kid, quiet, kind of a strange bird. I don't think he got out much, if you know what I mean. Like I mentioned before, in Mick's suite there were all these beautiful pieces of artwork, and I'm sure Peter thought nobody would notice, so he snatched a small piece off the wall and stuffed it in his luggage.

Anyway, they get to Customs in Rome, and the officers are asking all the questions, like: "Anything you'd like to claim? Do you have anything that doesn't belong to you? Did anyone give you anything?"

These Customs guys are riffling through people's shit like nobody's business. They're opening all of Dennis, Rick, and Lou's suitcases. They're opening their wives' stuff, and touching everything: powder puffs, underwear, whatever they can get their hands on. The fellas are getting a little upset and rightfully so, but guess who's being quiet the whole time? Peter Reilich. He's just standing there, saying nothing, turning white as a ghost, as he inches closer to his turn for Customs to check his bags.

"What is this?" one of the officers asks Peter, pulling the stolen piece from his suitcase.

The kid, being the way he was, crumpled. The rest of the band is looking at him, wondering what the hell was going on, and suddenly Peter is taken away in handcuffs.

They held everyone at the airport. It would be several long hours before everyone was informed that Mr. Reilich would not be entering the country. You see, they don't take art theft lightly in Europe. In fact, it's such an egregious offense that it triggered Interpol. Peter was on his way back to France. Room and board would still be free, but this time it would be in a French jail.

Needless to say, Bobby and I were stunned. Nobody was really talking about it, and there wasn't much to say. The mood was somber, confused, and downright gloomy. People left the dinner and went their separate ways.

But after everyone had gone to their rooms, Bobby and I stayed behind. He gave me that look again, and minutes later, *Oh, the streets of Rooooome!*

Those Vespas sure can rip.

Later that night, Bobby and I found ourselves back inside the gates of the Vatican. There's like this holy circle in there that you can loop, and we'd been there in the afternoon on the mopeds and didn't realize that at a certain time, of course, there's a curfew. I'm sure there's probably a sign that says "No Admittance" after such and such a time. Now it's 11:30, 12 at night, and we're riding around on mopeds like we own the joint.

Out of nowhere, we're stopped by these two burly-looking Vatican Guards holding automatic weapons. I'm like, *Holy fuck! These guys are pointing Uzis at me!*

I might've been a little overdramatic, but I was also a little high. Plus, coming off that story about Peter getting arrested and taken back to France . . . well, let's just say, it felt like these guards weren't about to give Bobby and me the keys to the city.

"Passoporto! Passoporto!"

And of course, we didn't have our passports on us because we didn't think we'd need them. I start yammering, "Americanos! Friends! Amigos?"

And Bobby's Italian is even worse than mine, "Speci . . . gioto . . . Vespa . . . musico . . ."

These two guards looked like we were insulting their mother tongue, which to be fair, we kind of were. And I think I noticed their Uzis lifting in my direction.

"Foreigner! Bando! Urgent-o!" I pleaded. And then—and I still don't know what came over me—I just started to sing in this broken, scared voice, "I've been waiting . . ."

Bobby joined right in with the harmony, "For a girl like you . . ."

And all together now: "*TO COME INTO MY LIFE!!*"
The guards both softened, and their guns lowered.
"*I'VE BEEN WAITING FOR A GIRL LIKE YOU . . .*"
They bopped their heads and smiled.
"Ahh! Musica!" one of them said.
"Yes! Yes!" I replied. "Musica!"

And it was over. Just like that. Who knows what would have happened and what kind of trouble we might've been in. I mean, we'd likely been up for forty-eight hours straight at that point. We couldn't have looked like the most trustworthy duo of all time, but music—sweet, sweet music—saved the day once again. We were gonna be okay, at least for one more night.

Left: On the Telecaster and singing backup with bass player Rick Wills. Savannah Civic Center, March 16, 1982. (Credit: Lynn Heydenreich) *Below:* On the backline with Peter Reilich and the ultimate sideman, Bobby Mayo. South Bend, Indiana, December 13, 1981. (Credit: Lynn Heydenreich)

Right: A sideman has to be able to do it all: With Foreigner's Mick Jones. Syracuse, NY, April 3, 1982. (Credit: Lynn Heydenreich) *Below:* Picking up the slack: Soundcheck with Bobby Mayo (cigarette) after keyboardist Peter Reilich's sudden departure from the band. Orchard Park, NY, July 3, 1982. (Credit: Lynn Heydenreich)

18

PING-PONG

We had a nice weekend. The weather didn't want to cooperate, but Sandra and I played ping-pong. Sandra loves playing ping-pong. We went to our friends' house before all of this virus shit, and they have a pretty expansive basement with a full-on ping-pong table with the rubber floor and all that.

Anyway, Sandra saw that and lit up like a Christmas tree. And I was like, "Ping-pong? Really? That's what does it for you?"

So, we ended up buying one and I put it together. It took me like a whole day just to figure out the legs. But now, every day at about five o'clock, she says, "Are you up for a game?"

And part of me is like, "Nah, I don't really want to play," but as soon as we pick up the paddles and have our first couple of volleys, she starts beaming like a nine-year-old. She's like jumping up and down. So how can you say no? It's very therapeutic.

Sandra and I met in 1982 while I was on tour with Foreigner on their *4* record. We were in Basel, Switzerland, and the photographer Hannes Schmid–famous for the iconic Marlboro Man shot and the premier rock 'n' roll photographer in Europe at the time—introduced us. There was a big Atlantic Records dinner and Sandra was sitting across from me, and I'm like, "Wow!" and totally hitting on her. But she wanted nothing to do with me because Hannes and his girlfriend, Susie, had told her, "By the way, Mark's a great guy, but he's got a lot of girlfriends, so you don't want to get too get involved with him."

She wouldn't even look over at me. Evidently, she'd just broken up with a guy, so she wasn't exactly primed to be swept off her feet. I did, however, manage to get the phone number of the shop where she was a hair stylist, and I kept calling the shop, but she'd never come to the phone. And I finally called Susie, her girlfriend, and said, "Susie, I'm trying to reach Sandra and invite her out to a show. We're going to be in Nice and we have five days off."

Well, that seemed to do the trick because Sandra finally answered the phone and flew out to France a few days later. We were in this amazing hotel called Le Negresco, and the second day we were together, I called my mother, who stuttered when she was nervous, and she goes, "Where are you, dear?"

I said, "I'm in Nice, Ma."

And my mom started stammering, "That's Fra-Fra-France is very expensive."

And I said, "Mom, it's cool. Don't worry about it. But Mom, I want you to say hello to the woman that I want to marry."

And I gave Sandra the phone with my mother probably still stuttering, and Sandra goes, "Hello?" in her Swiss accent.

So that's how I proposed, and fortunately, Sandra didn't say no.

Forty years later, we still like each other. We still hold hands and say "I love you" before going to bed. That's not typical in rock 'n' roll, where it seems like it's easier to go on the road and say, "Fuck it, I give up," when faced with the pitfalls of marriage. Sure, there are times when we clash, but it always works out. Like, whenever I leave the house, be it for ten minutes to go grab some milk or two months to go out on tour, I'll beep the horn three times as I make my way down the driveway. It's just something I always do. Even if I'm frustrated at something, like maybe she wouldn't let go of something or she harped on something or I expected something, whatever it is, and I'll leave and slam the door. But I'll still "beep, beep, beep" to let her know I'm not that mad. And by the time I'm on the highway, I'll call her.

Two things I know: you don't go to bed angry, and you don't leave someone where anything can happen in the world without telling them you love them.

■ ■ ■

As a kid, my father showed me the rewards of being a family man. Of being a good husband and father. He showed me that a father is willing to sacrifice everything for his family so that they might know happiness and grow up strong.

But how would that work if I was a music man? Even to this day, when my two boys are all grown and out living adult lives of their own, that question can feel unresolved. Did I give them and Sandra everything they needed? Because now, looking back, it's impossible for me not to see the young adult I was, striving so hard to achieve my dreams in music, without appreciating its implications for my future family. I was making choices long before they came into my life that would affect them as much, if not more, than me.

The fact is, a musician earns as he works, and while I'm grateful for that opportunity, there are dark periods when there's no work. That never goes away.

Back in the mid '90s, after years of successful tours and gigs, things dried up for a while. A long while. And I was scrounging. I mean, I would drive down to these little songwriting gigs in Jersey in hopes that maybe we'd write a hip song. I was so broke that I'd drive up to these tollbooths on the Garden State Parkway, and I'd slow down and scrounge for the quarters people dropped. That's how broke I was.

One time, a cop saw me and pulled me over. He said, "You know, I can give you a $50 fine, which would be a lot worse."

And with tears in my eyes, I said, "Officer, you have no idea. I don't do this because I'm trying to beat the system. I have nothing right now."

The guy looked at me, and I could see that he knew I wasn't bullshitting, and he just said, "Go on." He didn't even say don't do it again. He just told me to get home safe.

That was thirty years ago, so our oldest was about six and his brother three, and I'm thinking, *Fuck, I can't even pay a toll.*

And I'm driving down to NJ to write songs because I think we're going to have a hit and I think a song might maybe make me a gazillion dollars, so I never have to worry about money again. That was the dream. But with a family in tow, the dream got to wear a bit thin because you can't feed a family off of dreams. And when I got home that evening, it was after midnight and I rolled up the driveway slowly and tried to come in the house and into bed quietly, and I don't know how—Sandra has this sense or this perception that she knows when something is wrong—but she woke up and asked, half asleep, "Are you alright?"

And I broke down and told her, "I got pulled over by a cop," and she's thinking, "Oh God, you lost your license," and I said, "No, no, I had to pick up change."

She held me and said we're going to get through this. The next day, she started cutting hair again.

I was told long ago that in order for a relationship to be successful, there's a certain amount of work that needs to be done, but it's not always 50/50. Sometimes, one person puts in more work than the other. But as long as 100 percent of the work is being done, then the relationship can endure. Well, in the Rivera household, that person is Sandra. She's my rock. I always say she's had to raise three boys, not just two. Because there were so many times that I thought we would lose the house and I started fretting about what would we do, thinking I'm a failure, and I'd come home and she'd be there, letting me know that no matter how bad shit was because I'd fucked up, or I should've saved more money, or I shouldn't have done drugs—whatever it might be—that we'd get through it together. And though I probably didn't deserve it, she provided solid footing. She provided the extra percent and we endured.

So, yeah, now we're stuck home and playing ping-pong all weekend. And I'm grateful for it. I mean here I am, twiddling my thumbs the last ten months (or however fucking long it's been), wondering when we're gonna get back on the road, and then you play some stupid game with your spouse and you smile and you laugh and you're like, "Oh yeah, I got all of this. Fuck music. It will come when it comes. Just enjoy this." Because God knows how many times I've wished for exactly these moments while I was on the road, where you spend five or six hours on the job, between the soundchecks and the actual show, and then the lights go down and the ringing is still going on in your ears, and you're either going to a bar and meeting friends and everything's so "groovy, groovy, groovy," and then you go to your room and you think, "Okay, where would I really like to be right now?" and the answer is always, "Home."

And that's the silver lining of all of this pandemic shit. Because when it comes down to it, the truth is everything else—the music and the good times—can go away as long as my family's all right. That's the bottom line. The fragility of all that is around us, and you start to realize, "Man, I am the luckiest sonuvabitch alive." So what do you do? You put your dancing shoes on and play some ping-pong with the ones you love.

19

SOFT LANDING

In the late '70s and early '80s, we had all sorts of crises: energy, oil, the savings and loan collapse, inflation, the stock market. Unemployment was as high as 10 percent. Words like *recession* and *correction* peppered the newspapers. But by the end of 1982, we were starting to pull out of it.

Not that I was even aware.

I mean, you're talking to a guy who in the first part of 1980 was barely able to pay his phone bill. And when I started making dough, I still went from moment to moment and month to month. All this concern about the economy or the stock market, I was oblivious. Sure, I was making about $2,500 a week, which was certainly more than I ever imagined I'd make in my life, but money came in, money went out.

And it's crazy because I'm not sure what I would have done had the next gig not come along. By the time Foreigner's tour was wrapping up, I might've saved maybe five grand, which was sure to evaporate as soon as somebody called with one stupid idea or another . . .

■ **1982-1983**

Fortunately, the last couple of months with Foreigner provided a soft landing rather than a hard stop. We went from playing four shows a week, all over the globe, to weekend gigs mostly on the East Coast. That meant I could get back in the swing of things and ultimately land my next gig before losing a paycheck. So, if the band would do a Friday in Baltimore and then a Saturday night show in Philly, I'd be back in the city on Sunday for four or five days, planting seeds for my next gig.

I was back in the hustle—fortunately with a few weapons at my disposal.

The first was my little black date book. Talk about analog! But it was a good system. Red ink meant the gig was solid as a rock. Blue ink was like it was looking good, depending upon my schedule. And pencil was like, "Hey, we're thinking about doing something." If that something happened to go from pencil to blue ink, I'd just write over it. If it went from blue to red, I'd put a big circle around it in red. Lots of red meant I was solid for the week, otherwise I knew I had to shake the trees and land some more gigs.

My entire life was in those pages—every player, every producer, every studio, every club, every important date. I remember Jeff Golub, the guitarist for Billy Squier and Rod Stewart, offered to buy it from me. Jeff was a dear friend. And one day he saw me thumbing through my book, searching for this or that.

"I'll give you a thousand bucks," he said.

"For what?" I asked.

Jeff glanced at the book in my hands and said, "*You know what.*"

Now, why would a guy like Jeff Golub—a guy with such a heavy pedigree and probably all the same professional connections I had—offer *a thousand dollars* for my little black book? Because besides the industry contacts, I had a lot of ladies' numbers in there. (These were collected long before Sandra, of course.)

"A thousand bucks, right now," Jeff said, fishing around for his wallet.

I don't care if it's 1981 or 2021, a thousand bucks is a lot of money.

But I said, "Take any phone number you want, buddy, but no sale. *Not a chance.*"

It was too important. Lots of people had managers and agents to do their booking, but as far as I could see, they weren't getting any more dates than I was getting on my own, yet they were giving up fifteen percent of their paycheck. I won't say I was a "hot commodity" or anything, but with Foreigner's *4* under my belt, I was now a guy with some juice. People associated me with Junior Walker and his solo on "Urgent." And if I could play that solo every night, then they figured, *This Mark guy's the real deal*, and would call me up.

So, an agent was unnecessary. I had credentials, my little black book, and, to tie it all together, a call service. Radio Registry. Everybody and their brother used them.

Radio Registry basically existed so that producers and other people could track you down. For example, I did a lot of studio sessions for Jimmy Biondolillo, a big film and TV arranger, out at Media Studios. If Jimmy wanted to get in touch, he'd call Radio Registry. I'd get the message and call him back.

"What's up, Jimmy?" I'd ask from wherever the hell I was.

"Hey, when are you back in town?"

And maybe I'd reply, "Two days."

Jimmy would say, "Great, I'll hold the session up for you."

That may seem like no big deal, and I'm sure this must be such a foreign concept to anyone under forty years old. But thanks to the call service, I had gigs like Jimmy's lined up all the time. It was like your very own personal receptionist, and it was a godsend for anyone in the business trying to make a living.[1]

Mind you, I wasn't the highest roller on the studio circuit. I mean it's New York City in the early '80s. So, we're talking about Michael Brecker, David Sanborn, and many others. But there was still a lot of work. Because those guys easily demanded double or triple scale. So, for them to come in and play a solo, it might cost someone a thousand dollars. Whereas if I came in, it cost about three hundred, three-fifty.

The producer would say, "Well, for three hundred and fifty bucks, I'll pay you in cash."

Now we're both happy.

I remember Jimmy connected me with a couple of women who had a group called Two Tons O' Fun. They were best known for recording that song "It's Raining Men" as the Weather Girls. There was an agent involved on their end, and he wanted to know if I was gonna be cool when I got in the studio—you know, that I wasn't going to be tripping about how long the session might go. A lot of guys come in and are like, "Hey man, I'm looking at my watch. I've got a two o'clock session. This can't go more than an hour and a half."

---

1. Not surprisingly, Radio Registry was started by a receptionist. Doris Sharpe began working as one in 1930 for CBS in their radio department. She identified the need for radio actors to be able to locate work and get booked on jobs even while they were busy on other gigs. In 1938 she started the service with her life savings of $300. Soon, nearly every radio actor and performer had the same contact number on their business cards: "Lackawanna 4-1200, Radio Registry." Doris Sharpe died a very wealthy woman. (Source: Jack French, "The Little Lady Who Could Locate Anybody: Doris Sharpe of Radio Registry," Metropolitan Washington Old Time Radio Club, 2004, http://www .mwotrc.com/rr2005_02/registry.htm)

Well, that's not me. I go into that room with the Two Ton gals, and I'm like, "Hey, if it takes two hours, four hours, you're gonna pay me three hundred bucks and we're cool. And we'll have lunch." It's a lot easier for a guy to get along with people when you're not looking at your watch, hopping to the next studio gig.

So that was the studio scene. But even when I was off the road, I'd spend most of my time playing live gigs. That was my scene and, not surprisingly, where I caught my next big break.

■ ■ ■

David Brown played the guitar on the demos of Cash, which became Tycoon, and seven years later I found myself playing with him in between Foreigner weekends in a band called the Late Boys. David was a real player—he had a great feel—so it was no wonder he was a staple in Billy Joel's band.

One night we're playing at a club called My Father's Place.[2] It was a legendary joint on Long Island that had featured thousands of acts and performers all trying to take the step, including the Police, Madonna, Eddie Murphy, and Andy Kaufman. And on this particular night, our band was undeniable. David was playing monster guitar solos, and the material was so deep. We'd play Little Feat, Sly, Hendrix. It was so eclectic and electric. Little did I know that Richie Cannata, Billy Joel's saxophonist, was sitting in the crowd. I couldn't have picked him out if he'd been sitting front and center. I'm sure David invited him or maybe mentioned that he was playing with some *other* sax player or something. I don't really know.

At the intermission, David introduced us.

---

2. According to the *New York Times*, My Father's Place "created a scene that would influence music for decades to come." (Robbie Woliver, "Working in the Spirit of My Father's Place," *New York Times*, 2000, https://www.nytimes.com/2000/08/27/nyregion/working-in-the-spirit-of-my-father-s-place.html)

I said, "Hey, man, it's a pleasure to meet you." I reached out my hand, but it wasn't met with the same enthusiasm, if you know what I mean. Maybe he was a little more impressed than he wanted to be. I mean, I was having a night. I was like a cross between James Brown and Jimi Hendrix on the saxophone. And let's be honest, Richie's an incredible player, but it's strictly saxophone. Richie did not sing. Richie did not dance.

Anyway, the world works in mysterious ways because a week or so later, we're doing another gig and David again pulls me aside. This time he says, "So, Richie and Billy are parting ways and Billy's looking for a sax player." He then asked if I'd be interested.

Foreigner and now maybe Billy Joel? Holy shit!

A few days later, David connected me with Doug Stegmeyer, Billy's bass player and musical director. The idea was that if he liked me, I would try out for Billy and the whole band. So, I took the alto sax for the train ride on the Long Island Railroad out to Doug's place, and when I arrived at his stop in Huntington, Doug was there waiting to pick me up.

Everything about the guy was relaxed and low key. We even grabbed a slice before heading to his house, where he had a small studio down in the basement. He just wanted to hear that I at least had a decent tone. Because up until that time, he had never even heard of me. So he puts on "Just the Way You Are" and I'm playing, and I can tell he's into it because he's smiling and moving his head to the music.

The song ends and Doug goes, "It's gonna go great," and drives me back to the station. That was it. The whole trip was maybe an hour and a half, including lunch.

■ ■ ■

Before parting ways, Doug handed me a couple of Billy Joel cassettes—*The Stranger* and *Turnstiles*. He said something like,

"Go home. Listen to 'Just the Way You Are,' 'Only the Good Die Young,' and 'Say Goodbye to Hollywood.' And learn the background vocals." That was the assignment.

I didn't really know Billy's music very well. When he came out with the album *Piano Man* in 1973, I'd had friends rave about it, but I was still way into louder, heavier stuff like Hendrix and Cream. The song "Captain Jack" might come on with the line "You just sit at home and masturbate," and I'd say, "What the fuck is this?" Billy and singer-songwriters in general weren't my speed. And sure, he'd been all over the Top 40 for a decade since, and maybe it's not a great thing to say as a musician, but I wasn't paying attention to the radio back then. First off, I didn't have a car, so there was that. But even if I was in a car with one of my buddies, we'd pop in someone like Procol Harum or the Rascals.

But now I was being properly introduced. Of course, the first song—"Just the Way You Are"—had been playing on the airwaves for several years by that point. Even a non-radio guy like me knows that song, and when I started to play it, I realized that I had sort of learned that tune by osmosis.

The other two tunes—"Only the Good Die Young" and "Say Goodbye to Hollywood"—had solos and vocals to learn. I listened and was figuring them out. That's all I really paid attention to. You know, you're playing, you put that cassette player on, you have the sax part in hand. You're playing back and forth, and you want it to be just right. And by about a day or two into it, I wore those cassette tapes out. See, the last thing you wanna do at any time while you're playing music is to think about what the music requires of you. Because if you're thinking about what's required of you, you'll probably spend more time thinking about it than actually doing it. Your music has to be second nature.

And it didn't hurt that I was becoming inspired by the music. It was the first time I really allowed myself to get intimate with

Billy's sound. *Oh, this is what my friends liked so much* . . . So, by the time the audition came, I was like, *pfft*—I got this. Again, not arrogance, just confidence. *I got this.* But what I was not prepared for was how incredible these guys were live. It was hands down the best band I'd ever sat in with.

■ ■ ■

When you play with a drummer who puts the backbeat where you are comfortable, it's like putting on a nice old jacket or pair of jeans that feel good to wear. You can buy a new leather jacket, but it won't feel like the old bomber jacket. Liberty DeVitto, the drummer, and Doug Stegmeyer, the bassist, put the pocket where you wanted to have it. And they were a great complement to each other. Liberty absolutely pounded the drums—*hard and with passion.* And Doug played these amazing, beautiful cello lines: very lyrical, to go with a bottom end that he held down like no one else. And the combination of those two guys created this incredibly strong foundation. *Who wouldn't want to play with that beneath their feet?*

We started with "Only the Good Die Young" and "Say Goodbye to Hollywood" and it's amazing because I was basically just sitting in with this band, trying out, and within the first couple of minutes I felt like I'd been there forever. We were like this seven-tentacled unit that would go faster when it needed to, pull back when it needed to. We were all glued together. It felt so right.

The vibe was incredible. I knew I had shattered that shit. Again, not arrogant, but confident. I came prepared because I didn't want to disappoint myself. Truth was, you could read it all over these guys' faces—they were digging it, too.

We closed the three-song set with "Just the Way You Are." I thought I was nailing it, but right after the solo, Billy stopped the band and I was like, *oh shit, did I fuck up??*

150

Billy stood up and walked over to me. He looked at me with his big warm eyes and said, "Come here." He pulled me in close and kissed me on the cheek. He said, "As long as you want a spot in my band, you got it."

Phew!

The band gave me a warm welcoming applause, while Liberty rang his cymbals. I was officially Billy Joel's saxophonist.

Live at Shea Stadium with special guest Tony Bennett,
who describes Billy Joel as "the walking American
songbook." July 16, 2008. Welcoming me into the
band in 1982, Billy offered what's turned out to be
the gig of a lifetime. (Credit: Kevin Mazur)

WORKING-CLASS BAND

■ **1982**

With the Foreigner tour, I was eating lobster and caviar and drinking champagne every night because Atlantic Records thought the sun set up the band's ass. That's how it was. Foreigner *4* was their golden goose. They got tons of airplay and the label was making so much money they couldn't do enough for us. It was excessive. It was gluttonous . . .

But that wasn't the case with Billy Joel's tour. First, *The Nylon Curtain* wasn't a smash. Compared to Billy's previous albums, it was a flop. The man sold records—at least four or five million records right behind this one—but *The Nylon Curtain* took a while to go gold, let alone platinum.

I thought the record was fantastic, but the point I'm making is that Columbia Records wasn't putting out a lot of big dinners for us. Sure, the company would take Billy out once in a short while, but the whole band wasn't invited, if you catch my drift. Compared to Foreigner, it was a lot leaner.

But it wasn't just dollars and cents; Billy ran a different operation. I remember there was this Thanksgiving dinner. The whole crew was there, and it was a bunch of turkey and stuffing and whatever. Family style. When it was over, there was some food left, and Billy insisted that we wrap up sandwiches for the plane the next day. And I was thinking, *Whoa, leftovers?* Because that was not the mentality I'd grown accustomed to. I mean, if it was a Foreigner gig, that turkey and stuffing and cranberry would be in the trash five minutes after the band left the room. The amount of food they threw out at the end of any given night could've fed a small village.

Anyway, that plane ride with the turkey sandwiches will never leave my head. Sandra talks about it to this day.

She'd come over from Switzerland to visit—we still hadn't set a date for the wedding—and mid-flight Billy walked up as though he was our server. He was in first class, and I think we were in coach because there wasn't enough room for both Sandra and me up front. But it didn't matter, because here comes Billy Joel slouching his way down the main cabin holding this cardboard box full of turkey sandwiches. He approaches us like a waiter out of a black-and-white movie and asks, "Sandra, my dear, what would you like to order? How about turkey? Yeah, you want the turkey."

And he just hands Sandra a leftover sandwich. Doesn't even give her time to answer. She's holding this limp sourdough thing with both hands palms up, and it's hilarious. She can't stop laughing, and then he turns to me, "And what about you, sir?"

Billy looks me up and down, playing it so cool. "Would you like something to eat? How about turkey. Yeah, you want turkey too, sir."

He drops me a sandwich, hamming it up all the way. We're hysterical. Everyone around us is falling to pieces. Billy Joel is forcing Thanksgiving leftovers on everyone around him, and it's tremendous. There's not a dry eye on the flight.

And I'll tell you, it was at that moment that I remember thinking that I'd found something special. I mean I was a significant part of Foreigner's greatest tour, but when I started playing with Billy, I joined a family. I was a part of something, and we could laugh and take the piss out of each other and share each other's pain, even share Thanksgiving leftovers, in the way that you only do when you're a real family.

■ ■ ■

The reason people go see a show is because the music resonates on some level. Maybe they hear some catchy songs on the radio and when they hear the songs live and see the band in person, they freak out, like, "Oh my God, oh my God, oh my God . . ." That's the way it was with Foreigner. People freaked, and anywhere the band went, onstage or offstage, they always seemed like rock gods.

But other times, music touches something deeper. There's this more personal connection with it. And when the audience hears it live, it's not like they're looking up on stage at some superstar— they're way past the whole celebrity thing. They're looking up at an old friend. That's the first thing I noticed out on tour with Billy Joel. Even when the music was pumping and the crowd was dancing and singing and we were going nuts up onstage, there was always this intimate connection to the fans with Billy and his music.

I remember we were playing a show in Bethlehem, Pennsylvania, and when we played "Allentown," the place went crazy. You could just tell they felt like they were part of something, or Billy and the rest of us were a part of them. It was a working-class crowd being celebrated by a working-class piano man and his working-class band.

Originally, I didn't have much to do on that particular song except sing backup and a little percussion. But back at rehearsals, I too had been sucked up in the power of the song and I'd seen a metal pipe laying in the corner. So, while we were running through the song, I just picked up the pipe and started banging on it, like it was one of my percussion toys. I did it on a lark, but Billy loved it and we incorporated it as part of the act. Again, the song spoke to my blue-collar roots. My dad had worked the midnight shift. Hell, my grandfather lost a hand at a chocolate factory. And all the dads in my neighborhood were blue-collar guys.

And now, in Bethlehem, we were like thirty shows in, and the pipe had become a featured part of what we did. And at the end of the song, I picked up the pipe like a "Fight the Power" kind of thing, holding it up like you'd hold up a championship belt or the Stanley Cup. I held it up and the people were like, "Yeah! Fuckin' A! We bang steel! We're Pennsylvania!"

Sometimes I'm recognized as "that guy who bangs the pipe on 'Allentown.'" I'm good with that. So good. I mean, I obviously had the sax and all the great bits that I got to do. But it was something that stood out. I think it was really the beginning of my being more of a showman. Everything up until that time was me just playing, just performing. But at that point, I realized I had more of a theatrical thing that I could contribute.[1]

And that's the power of Billy's writing. As a musician, as a fan, you can't help but get sucked up into the bigger picture. Especially "Goodnight Saigon" and "Allentown." These really resonated on that tour and in places like Bethlehem where you got the feeling

---

1. I remember some years after that all started, I did a gig with Jeff Kazee (Bon Jovi, Southside Johnny), who's since become a dear friend and bandmate, and after the gig Jeff was so excited to get home so he could tell his wife, "Hey, Constance! I just had a gig with the guy who plays the pipe in 'Allentown'!"

that the men in the audience came home covered with soot and needed a shower and a beer, as opposed to their bedroom slippers and a martini. There were guys that were just out of the Vietnam War a couple of years, and people in neighborhoods that were full of kids who'd been drafted and shipped off to the war. These weren't college-deferment kids. These were kids from neighborhoods like Brooklyn and Queens and the Bronx.

And up on stage it was a very blue-collar mindset, too. Very egalitarian, as in "we're all in this together." I mean, take the way we were set up on stage. I had a place that was visible the whole time. We all did. I'd interact with Liberty. I'd interact with David Brown. I'd interact with Billy. We played off of him and he played off of us. It was like going back to Trax, playing with those guys like Yogi and Bett. It was just jamming with the band. Again, I never really got that with Foreigner. There wasn't that sort of community and synergy.

I mean, nobody in Foreigner really moved. Lou had one move: back and forth. He sang great, but he wasn't a great entertainer. And Mick was a terrific guitarist, but he didn't exactly run around. Whereas I could be more of a showman. I mean, people used to come see me play, even going back to Maitrex Square or Pecker Frost and the Battle of the Bands where you had to bring your A-game to the stage, and they'd say, "You're a showman." But on songs like "Urgent," it was clear that the sax solo was going to be a showpiece because that solo was so separate from anything else in that set. It was undeniable. They couldn't have me playing that solo from back behind the stacks. So, I'd come down and play the solo, and then go back to the risers tucked in the back. And I think that was very much by design. It was almost like, "Thank you, Mark. You can go now."

But Billy wasn't like that. He *wanted* others to shine. For me, that meant probably eight sax solos, big vocal parts, the pipe, the triangle in Saigon. *Ding!* And that may seem like a silly thing, but it's quite special theatrically. There's a penlight on Billy's piano and another one overhead on me playing a triangle. And yeah, I wasn't being asked to play a keyboard in one hand and a sax in the other like I was with Foreigner, but I was out front, and it was a leap in my performance, or my identity. Because "Urgent" was great. It was so frickin' bombastic, the whole thing. And frankly, as much as it was a showpiece and exhilarating to do, I didn't hear a fucking thing I played. It was so loud down front: Mick Jones's guitar, and Rick's bass, and the snare drum, and the wedges in those side fills. It was so overbearing. I could never hear myself down there. Whereas with Billy, I was back in the Trax mode, and I could hear the music and really get connected to what I was doing.

And, again, he was confident in his playing and songwriting. Why would he not allow the rest of us to help him out? When we'd do "Italian Restaurant," for example, we'd set up a restaurant scene behind Billy, playing the piano. The place would be dark except for a spotlight on Billy. And it would just be him and the piano, and he'd sing the first line—*A bottle of red, a bottle of white*—and then behind him, a second spotlight showed the table. And there'd be four of us acting out the scene: Russell, David Brown, myself, and Liberty. We weren't playing any instruments because Billy would carry the whole first part, and we'd be sitting around the table and someone in the crew would play the waiter. It was like four guys from the old neighborhood sharing a meal, breaking bread together and having a good time. It was so simple, but people couldn't take their eyes off of us. It worked perfectly. Steve Cohen, the lighting director, lit the table and these four knuckleheads, goofing around. And we were always hamming it up. We would have fun. And the audience would respond and Billy would have to look back, like, *What are these idiots doing now?*

But he never once said, "You guys are stealing my thunder." He never once said, "Hey, could you guys back off a little bit?" He *loved* it and encouraged us to have fun. His whole mindset was whatever the band or the crew needed to do to support the song, we should do it. He just seemed to love people interpreting his music and performing.

There was one night, early on in that first tour, when the whole PA system went out. Everything just stopped. The guitars stopped and Liberty stopped banging on the drums. Most guys would say, "Okay, that's it," and go off stage until the crew got things working again. But not Billy. He said, "Hey, hold on a second." And he starts playing "Always a Woman." The crowd of twenty-some-thousand people fell absolutely silent. Fans in the nosebleeds could probably barely hear him, but Billy starts belting it out to the back of the arena. It was so magical. So intimate. By the end of the song, people in the audience are holding up lighters and swaying back and forth in unison. And the sound they made when he hit the final notes. Things might let you down in this world—the electricity goes out, your job stinks, maybe there's even an act of God—but not tonight, not Billy Joel. My God, what an amazing moment. To think the sonuvabitch could handle that with no problem. Just a piano, a voice, and an arena full of jaw-dropped fans and band members.

The audience loved him. Every place we went, you kept waiting for the other shoe to drop—"Oh, we're gonna have a real stinker here." Because a bad show is inevitable. But not this band. Every place, they loved us. And we crisscrossed the United States. Every one of them was so well received. Like I said, you just think, "One of these days we're gonna have a real stinker."

But it never happened.

Part of the reason for that was we all got along. From the band to the crew, there was a special bond. We were mostly New

Yorkers, from the same neighborhoods—sometimes it felt like the same block. We had blue-collar fathers and blue-collar uncles and blue-collar cousins. We may have slung instruments instead of hammers, but we never forgot where we came from. And of course, there's a whole language that comes with that. Growing up in Brooklyn, we called it Brooklynese, but it was pretty much the same in all of the boroughs. A lot of *fuck this* and *fuck that* and *fuhgeddaboudit*.

It makes me think of one moment that happened early on. We were playing the Nassau Coliseum, and Vinny DeVitto, Liberty's brother, came up to us backstage before the show.

"This fuckin' guy," he says. Liberty and his brother grew up in Queens and it's always *this fuckin' guy*. "I'm trying to park, and this fuckin' guy comes up and says, '*Fivedollahs*.'"

We're already laughing.

"He says, '*Fivedollahs*.' So, I tell this guy, 'I'm fuckin' Liberty DeVitto's brother. Where do I park?' This guy just looks at me and says, '*Suck my wad. Fivedollahs*.'"

Well, of course we all fell over laughing. And the line stuck. We'd say it for the rest of the tour. Ask for a beer? "*Suck my wad. Fivedollahs*." Think you deserve a hotel upgrade? "*Suck my wad. Fivedollahs*." Looking for the set list? "*Suck my wad. Fivedollahs*."

I'm sure that sounds kind of stupid, but when you're out on the road, bouncing from one station to the next, it's nice to be surrounded by that level of familiarity, regardless of how juvenile. Again, *family*. It lets you laugh and never take yourself too seriously, no matter if you were *the guy*, Billy, or just one of the guys driving the trucks. You felt included and part of something you innately understood. And when you can share a laugh together, it makes the whole journey more relaxed and things keep moving with positive energy.

There were other in-jokes, of course, plenty of them. One that stands to this day is *"Nuns,"* which simply means *shutthefuckup.*

This happened before I joined the band, and I heard it a couple of times before it was explained to me by Steve Cohen, the brilliant lighting director. What happened was Billy had a couple of drinks in the hotel bar and was hanging out with Steve and Brian Ruggles, the equally brilliant sound director. So, they leave the bar and Billy gets into the elevator, facing away from the door while he's talking to Steve and Brian. And he's going, *Fucking guy this. Fuck fuck fuck.*

And then Steve looked Billy straight in the eyes and said, "Nuns."

Billy was like, "What the fuck you talkin' about?"

Steve motioned behind Billy and repeated, *"Nuuuns."*

As it turns out, there were two actual nuns in full habits walking onto the elevator right behind Billy, who's still cursing like a scene in a Mob movie. Finally, he got the message, and he turned around.

"Oh, good evening, ladies . . ."

Nuuuns. It's part of our language.

First gig after 9/11 (note the fireman's helmet on Billy's piano). Billy's music continues to meet the moment, healing and inspiring people—including his sax player—in ways that very few, *if any*, artists can. (Credit: © Voyages, Inc.)

21

BE COOL

What does it take to be a sideman? I've never really thought about it before in concrete terms because it's not like I set off on this journey saying, "I'm gonna be a sideman." It just sort of happened and like anything else, I got better at it as I went.

Any successful sideman will tell you there are three basic prerequisites to the job. One, you gotta have the chops—there's no hiding on stage, and if you can't bring the goods, everyone in the building is gonna know it. Two, when you're offstage, you gotta be a good hang. Nobody wants to be tripping around the globe with some stick in the mud or high-maintenance pain in the ass. Three, you gotta have a look. What that look is depends on the gig—sometimes it's punk, or maybe it's a Talking Heads gig and you gotta look strange as fuck. But everyone knows what rock 'n' roll is not. It's not boring. It's certainly not square. And if you can meet that standard, the front guys might cut you a little bit of slack on the look so long as you've got the chops and are a good hang. Those first two are the most crucial.

There's this great story that Daryl Hall and John Oates tell about auditioning the bass player, Tom "T-Bone" Wolk, for their (at the time) upcoming Private Eyes tour. Now, T-Bone was really a multi-instrumentalist and had already cracked a lot of the New York City studio session and jingle scene. But when you're Daryl Hall and John Oates in the 1980s, you can be picky.

So, they're down to the last couple of candidates when T-Bone walks into the rehearsal space. Now T-Bone's a great player but he's not exactly a heartthrob. And he's wearing this cap because T-Bone always wore a hat to conceal the top of his dome, which was as bald as a cue ball. And along with his bass guitar, T-Bone's carrying this accordion. *Why the fuck's he showing up to a rock gig with a fucking accordion?* And John jokingly asked, "Well, which one are you gonna play?"

T-Bone replied, "I'm gonna play the bass."

So anyway, T-Bone plays. He does his thing, which of course they love because playing bass just didn't get any better than what T-Bone was bringing, and they also dug his sort of low-key nature. This is not a guy who's gonna get on your nerves anytime soon. He's happy, he smiles, and most importantly he's super into and thoughtful about the music. And then he plays the accordion, and T-Bone was like the New York State champion on accordion by the time he was in the sixth grade. So he's incredible, and John and Daryl understand, "Okay, this is a serious musician."

So, T-Bone leaves and they've got one more candidate. And this last guy comes in and he's the whole rock 'n' roll package: he plays the bass great, he sings great, and he totally has the rocker look—long, skinny legs and long, blond, rock 'n' roll hair that the girls are all gonna lose their minds over. So that's the guy they give the gig to. Why? Because, again, the dude looked more rock 'n' roll.

But the story doesn't end there! Because when Daryl and John tell Mr. Long-Haired Rocker the gig's all his, the guy says,

"Okay, cool. But if I'm gonna do your show, I have to sing one song each night."

Of course, this takes Daryl and John by surprise. *Since when does a sideman sing the songs?*

So they ask him, "Well, which song did you have in mind?"

And the guy actually says, "I want to sing 'Kiss on My List.'"

Daryl and John just looked at each other like "What the fuck?" and said, "Let's call the bald guy with the accordion." Because immediately they figured this cat with the long hair had the potential to be a huge pain in the ass. I mean, who tells Daryl Hall, "I want to sing perhaps your most iconic song instead of you" and expects to keep the gig?

So, John and Daryl gave the spot to T-Bone, and for the next thirty years the funny-looking dude with the cap on his head became their go-to-guy, from playing bass guitar to very quickly becoming their musical director and playing wherever the hell else was needed—including, ladies and gentlemen, the accordion, which the band featured during its unplugged tour in the early '90s.

Anyway, I love that story.

■ 1983

Brian Ruggles and Steve Cohen, Billy's sound and lighting guys, had been talking me up to Paul Simon. They'd already done a couple of Simon & Garfunkel tours, so they knew Paul was looking for a new sax player. They mentioned to him that I got along with everybody, and that I had a real enthusiasm as a player. Like Billy, Paul wanted somebody who could fit in and not be awestruck.

I didn't even have to audition. Paul just showed up to one of our Madison Square Garden dates on the Nylon Curtain tour and told Brian and Steve that he loved the performance, loved the tone, and wanted me in the band. *Foreigner to Billy Joel to*

Simon & Garfunkel? This was becoming a little trippy. I mean, to land one or two of these gigs is more than most can hope for in a career. The fact that I'd gotten all of these in succession was beyond far out.

I was replacing Dave Tofani on saxophone. That was a huge compliment. Dave was part of the New York Saxophone Quartet, which is one of the most elite classical saxophone quartets out there. This was an international tour and a lot of these huge-deal guys didn't tour too much. They had their city gigs. They were making more money staying at home and playing sessions.

It's also noteworthy that Dave played the sax solo on "Still Crazy After All These Years."[1] And mind you, Gerry Niewood, who was the other saxophonist in the group, was a wonderful sax player. But Paul wanted me to do it. It was his way of saying, "Here, kid. Let's see what you can do." And if I had to guess, he was giving me the shot *not* because I was the better player, which I wasn't, but because of my performance abilities on stage. Part of it is how you play the notes, but the other part is how you present it, how you share the experience of it with the crowd and with your other bandmates.

I remember we were at SIR Studios for rehearsals and, after I took the solo, Paul turned and gave me a little smile. He's so understated. Just a smile and a nod. He has that loving, caring tone to him. Paul could simply say, "Hey, Mark," and it's like *I'm in.*

But it wasn't only Paul Simon that you worried about impressing. That whole band was ridiculous. It was a twelve-piece and everywhere you looked there were monsters. Richard Tee, musical director and keyboard player extraordinaire, was overseeing this

---

1. Including when Simon & Garfunkel performed and recorded their Central Park concert in 1981. Tofani, in turn, had replaced another saxophone legend, Michael Brecker, who'd performed the solo on the original recording.

crew. Carlos Vega was on drums. Carlos had already done tours. He'd been a hitmaking session guy on the West Coast. This guy Wayne Pedzwater was on bass. He had played with Buddy Rich and would go on to support Michael Jackson. Billy Payne from Little Feat was on the B-3, an absolute skull-crusher on the organ. Airto Moreira, the famous percussionist. All of these guys were the crème de la crème of the New York and L.A. session musicians.

Especially Richard Tee. The guy had played with everyone.

When I lived on Ninety-Seventh Street, I used to go to a place called Mikel's where Richard Tee's band, Stuff, played all the time. I probably saw them play thirty to forty times. And Tee, if he liked you, had a nickname for everybody. He called me "Stuffy."

Hey, Stuffy. Yeahhhh.

He was just one of those soulful cats that couldn't resist jiving even when the music wasn't playing. (You got the idea the music never ceased in Richard Tee's head.) Like when he met a woman that was like a big woman, but she had something going on, he said, "Yeah, she had *imperial* tonnage."

I still remember that. Tee had an expression for everything.

And Tee was a big man and a little intimidating. I mean the whole band's playing perfectly, but then a trumpet player might play one wrong note and Tee would look over and give that stink eye. And you'd be like, "Oh, boy. I fucked up."

But at the same time, when you did something well, like after a good solo, he'd smile and he'd go, "Yeah, Stuffy." And everything would be all right because Tee had a great smile, and he'd be playing along, that big body moving in time, swaying back and forth.

■ ■ ■

You always have someone in every band that you're best mates with. I had Bobby Mayo in Foreigner. I had Liberty with Billy. And I had Carlos Vega with Simon & Garfunkel. He was my accomplice, so to speak. We were inseparable. If we had a free minute during a duet where there was no percussion and no horn, you'd find the two of us smoking a joint together behind the bandstand.

The other band members, crème de la crème that they were, could be just so serious. And you got the idea that Paul liked to have these two younger idiots running around. We took our responsibilities seriously, but our laughter kept things light. Like during soundchecks, Art would always be picking the residual wig glue out of his hair from the night before. I mean everyone knew he wore a wig because he'd come out for soundcheck without it and be singing something like "Bridge over Troubled Water"—so serious and heartfelt—all the while sifting out glue globules from the back of his dome, rolling them between his fingers. It was so strange and of course Carlos and I would be semibaked and that was it. We couldn't stop laughing. Paul would understand what was going on and just have this tiny, understated grin on his face. Anyway, forty years later, I still can't hear "Bridge over Troubled Water," the duo's most soul-stirring song, without giggling a bit.[2]

I say that about Art, but it's amazing how cool those two guys were. Everyone wanted to hang with Paul and Art, and a lot of famous people came out to those shows. I remember one time Jack Nicholson was hanging out backstage, asking about Richard Tee's big piano case. See, Richard Tee played a proper acoustic piano, which meant every time it moved, it would have to be put in this giant case. I guess Jack saw that big-ass case and got curious.

So, he asked the piano tech, "Hey, do you have any of those packing blankets for that big piano case?"

---

2. And the song is obviously iconic. There's no escaping it in my business. Everyone and their brother has covered it, including Elvis Presley, Aretha Franklin, and Johnny Cash.

The tech guy replied, "Yeah, sure."

Jack goes, "I'll tell you what . . ." And Jack hands the tech the joint he was smoking. "I'm gonna go in that piano case. I'm gonna take a little nap."

So the tech opens the hatch and Jack climbs in, saying, "Make sure you wake me up before the last song of the set."

An hour or so later, the keyboard tech raps on the piano case, and Jack pops up, all refreshed. You can't make this stuff up.

But even with all the celebrities running around, sleeping in piano cases, the coolest dude was always Paul Simon. The man just exudes laid-back, *always* hip to the moment. And like Billy, he was totally open to suggestions and trying something new.

I'll give you two examples. First, for lack of a better phrase, there's a whistling solo on "Me and Julio" that Paul does. I remember Paul randomly turned to me once early on and said, "You don't have a big saxophone?"

I said, "I have a bass saxophone."

"A bass saxophone?"

There was always a little twinkle in Paul's eye when he was thinking something.

Paul made me schlep that bass sax all over the world and solo those whistles. *BUM BUH BUP BUH* . . . It was comical. But it was so completely different, and the crowd loved it.

Another time—this was actually during rehearsal—Paul asked me out of the blue what I thought about the horn parts on one song or another: "What do you think of these charts?"

And he had such a way of putting you at ease that I responded truthfully. I said, "I think they're kind of lame."

I wasn't saying it to be a wiseass, and he knew that.

And he said, "Well, what would you do?"

I said, "Well, how about this," and I just blew some lines without even thinking.

All of a sudden, some of the other guys are scribing these things down on notation paper. Paul loved it, and they became the parts.

That doesn't usually happen. But Paul is cut like that. He likes to keep it interesting.

■ ■ ■

On that tour, we had one of the first Steadicam operators. His name was Nicola Pecorini. He was an Italian camera operator, and the camera was very heavy, and it rested on his hips. And he would move around.

And I remember, he had a lazy eye. And everyone thought, *Must be difficult.*

But he said, "No, it makes it easier because I only use the one eye. Keeps it in focus and makes it easier to see what I'm doing."

Anyhow, Nicola was filming the close-ups and what he was seeing was projected onto the big screen for the whole audience. Since he had the Steadicam, he could come in and out and cruise all around the stage.

The entire horn section had stands for their sheet music. It looked very professional. But I didn't like sheet music and would just memorize the parts, so I'd throw a *Playboy* magazine up there for shits and giggles. Of course, from the crowd's perspective, it looked like I was reading music, studying intently as I played along. But when Nicola came around with the Steadicam, there was Miss July in her birthday suit up on the Teletron. The whole crowd got a peek.

I think it was Art who later said, "You'll have to avoid that in the future."

So, of course, I didn't do it again, but I had to laugh at the whole thing because it was like getting busted by my music teacher, Professor Cavolo, back in junior high. I mean here I was playing with perhaps the greatest band in the world, and I was still faking the whole reading-music bit. It was always that way with me. Playing from memory and by feel.

I would go on from here and continue my streak of playing with hot bands in the studio and out on hot tours. More Billy, more Simon & Garfunkel, more Foreigner. There would be new acts as well: Daryl Hall and John Oates, Billy and Elton John together on the Face to Face tours, Ringo Starr and His All Starr Band.

And in each of those gigs, there were times when I would realize something about my talent or its limitations. When I had to dig down a bit deeper and find something. But this moment with Simon & Garfunkel and that *Playboy* magazine sticks with me. Because if I could hang with these guys—take the big solos, have the balls to suggest changes to the horn parts—*and* do it with naked ladies on my music stand, then I'd figured something out. And whatever it was, it was working. It would keep on working.

And it's funny to think how this amazing journey on the big stage started in that stupid Latin band in the Catskills and my cousin Vinny introducing me to Bob Livingood, the trumpet player. It was Bob who got my foot in the door at the Record Plant, where I'd met my idol, John Lennon, joined Tycoon, and linked up with Mutt Lange. And it was Mutt who brought me to Foreigner, the very first of the big acts to take me out on the road. And sure, there were some dry patches these past forty years, times where no one was gigging and money was tight. But I've never had to call it quits. I've never really had to come off the road.

PART THREE

With Elton John at RFK Stadium, Washington, DC, July 20, 1994. Appropriately named Face to Face, the tour series paired together two titans—Billy Joel and Elton John—selling out stadiums worldwide for fifteen years. Pop charts may move on, but "classic rock" continues to be a fixture on the world's biggest stages, which is good news for the hustling sideman. (Credit: John L. Heithaus)

22

LIGHT AT THE END OF THE TUNNEL

Brewster, New York, 2021

Sandra and I were in Brooklyn last night. I had to drive down to pick up my saxophones, which had been baking in some truck in Nashville along with the rest of everyone's gear since the pandemic started. There are whispers that we might be coming out of this thing and getting back to playing shows. Nothing's scheduled, but I want the horns to be ready.

So, Sandra and I decided to make an evening of it and drive into the city. At least restaurants are back online.

We'd moved upstate immediately after our first baby, Derio, was born. 1984. It's funny because I'm the guy who always thought, *When I have a family, I'm gonna raise my kids in Brooklyn.* But six months after we got married, Sandra told me she was pregnant, and I did a complete one-eighty. *Wait, let the kid grow up in Brooklyn? In New York City? Are you nuts?!*

Because I saw the way guys like Lou Gramm lived. Upstate in the country. They had land. Space to grow. And I thought, *It's a no-brainer. I can teach my kids everything they need to know*

175

about Brooklyn and street smarts. So I started saying to Sandra, "We gotta get out of the city. We gotta buy a house."

And Sandra was more than fine with it. She's Swiss. She grew up in the Alps, like Heidi from *The Sound of Music.* She loves space.

The final push to move out to the country came when Sandra was in her third trimester. I was with Foreigner and we were off in Japan, and she went to the obstetrician for a checkup. And as she was leaving Central Park West, she saw a hand go around her neck. Some guy was trying to rip the necklace off of a seven- or eight-months-pregnant woman. She's leaving this beautiful door-man building, makes a left, and somebody rips her necklace off. So now, she's traumatized, four thousand miles away from home and the only person she knows—me—is in Japan. She didn't even get to tell me about that experience for like forty-eight hours because of the tour schedule!

And it's not like she was in the ghetto. I mean it's Central Park West! It's two blocks away from Paul Simon's apartment. It's six or eight blocks from the Dakota. It's lovely. But suddenly it goes to shit and you're like, "Okay, we definitely gotta get out of the city."

So we moved to the country, and we've been here for almost forty years.

But last night, even Sandra needed a little shot in the arm, so we headed into the big city to pick up my horns and grab some dinner. Shit, just sitting in traffic on the Van Wyck—the biggest clusterfuck ever—was a welcome change. It felt good to be part of the hustle and bustle again.

We arrived in Brooklyn, the old stomping grounds, to meet up with my very dear friend Mark Snyder, who was shepherding the horns (it was easier for Billy's crew to drop them with Mark than lug them all the way out to Brewster). I met Mark on the second Ringo Starr tour. He was Peter Frampton's guitar tech for years and actually helped develop the "Framptone," which is that voice box Peter features on a lot of his bigger hits, like "Show Me the Way" and "Do You Feel Like I Do?"

Mark is a brilliant guitar tech and a wonderful guitarist, but some years ago Mark came off the road and became a wine merchant. It's not rare for guys to discover their passion lies elsewhere, but he now owns Red Hook Winery in Brooklyn (the vineyards themselves are in the Finger Lakes region and Long Island's North Fork).[1] He's got an amazing nose. He could drink a glass of wine and tell you what was in the soil. It's pretty nuts how passionate the guy is about the craft.

So, Sandra and I met Mark and his beautiful family at Michael's Restaurant in Brooklyn. It's a great spot; Mark sells lots of wine to Michael's and he lives like three blocks away, so they gave us the presidential suite of outside dining. A big round table, right up front, tablecloths draped, and we were barely seated when Mark started ordering this and that and they started bringing out the wine and the appetizers. *Six appetizers.* Then the pasta. Three plates of pasta. After that, Mark was like, "Oh, we need chicken, we need a fish dish, pork, and, of course, we need a veal parmesan." The veal wasn't your typical veal parmesan. It was a pounded chop with the bone in and looked like a map of Australia. It was a mammoth.

But we all dug in. And seeing Mark—just feeling his passion for how food brings people together—made the table the happiest

---

1. David Lebolt, Billy's former keyboardist, is another example. David was a real techy guy. Like Mark, he eventually came off the road and moved out to San Francisco to work in the field of digital music. The guy became a superstar, guiding the development of Pro Tools, the industry-revolutionizing music software, and ultimately grabbing a 2004 Academy Award for Scientific and Technical Achievement in the process.

place in the world to be. It was less about sustenance for our bellies than for our souls.

■ ■ ■

When I'm out to dinner, it's not uncommon for someone to come up and ask, "Hey, are you Mark Rivera?"

And then I joke and say, "Why? Does he owe you money?"

But it's fun. I never want peace and quiet that much when I go out. And if anyone ever asks me to take a picture, and they ask, "Do you mind?" I say, "I would mind if you didn't ask me." Because I'm as happy to meet a person as hopefully they are to meet me. I really mean that. Music is about community and coming together. Being recognized is just part of that. And that's cool. Still, sometimes people linger, and that drives Sandra a little crazy.

Like last night, someone came up to the table and got kind of chummy. And to be fair, I had my saxophones, but he goes, "Hey, why don't you play 'New York State of Mind'?"

So I said, "Listen, I've been married thirty-seven years. If you want me to see thirty-eight, I'll play saxophone another time." In other words, I'm not doing the music stuff tonight. So, there's always a nice way to handle people who might press a bit too much.

But then, sometime after dessert, someone behind me exclaims, "Is that Mark Rivera?!"

I turn around, expecting to see someone I don't know, but it's a face from the old neighborhood, Neil Capone. I jumped up and immediately started giving Neil hugs and kisses, telling him, "Fuck social distancing."

Our families go way back. Neil's grandmother came over from the old country with my grandparents, and when they arrived at Ellis Island, they kissed each other goodbye, not sure if they'd ever see each other again. And somehow over the course of those first three years in America, my grandfather saved enough dough to buy a house. Twenty-five hundred cash. The house was originally double that, but it was the Great Depression, and I don't know what they did for food because they obviously didn't spend any money. So, they moved into the house and my grandmother's out sweeping her new steps and a woman comes out of the house next door, and lo and behold, it's Mrs. Danilo, my grandparents' companion on the trip to America. They'd bought houses next to each other, and for the next two generations, their kids and grandkids would all play and go to school together.

So, now I'm talking to Neil, the eldest brother of the three Capone boys—Burt, Neil, and the youngest, Steven. We're like family, and now Neil and I are reminiscing about the old days when we were all kids. "Remember your parties?" I asked him, and we both just started laughing.

Neil is like six years older than me, and when he was in high school, he would have these basement parties. He and his friends would be slow-dancing with girls, and they'd be grinding up against each other. And Neil's little brother Steven and I—we were always thick as thieves—we would be on our tippy toes looking over the frosted glass seeing what they were doing. It was like looking at a *Playboy* magazine, seeing these girls dancing. They're making out with their boyfriends, and it's all about who's grabbin' ass and who's grabbin' tit or whatever. And Neil saw what we were doing and kept yelling, "Get out of here!" He was always having to put up with Steven's and my shit.

Once, when Steven and I were a little pissed that Neil kept ruining the fun, the next morning we thought it was a good idea to play frisbee with his 45 records. These are Neil's favorite records, all the ones he'd been playing during his parties, and now we're down in the basement, trying to see who can fling the records harder. We probably shattered thirty records, maybe fifty, laughing as they'd explode against the wall.

Of course, Neil didn't think it was too funny at the time and he chased us around the block, but now, forty years later, he's got tears in his eyes as we're sitting around this table, reminiscing, laughing our asses off.

Anyway, it may not last forever, but you certainly can go home again, and the whole night—from getting my horns back to seeing good friends and being in the old neighborhood—it was the infusion that I needed so badly.

Later, on our way back to Brewster, Sandra goes, "Now you can sleep well tonight."

And it was true. I slept like a baby. And why not?

Things are starting to open up.

23

ALLOWING THE UNIVERSE TO UNFOLD

■ **Brewster, New York, 2021**

I'm very close with my dentist, Joel Himmelfarb. Great guy. He's a huge music fan and he came by yesterday and I said, "You want to have a beer?"

We sat outside and talked. And he said something really interesting. He goes, "When you speak about people, it's like the relationships that you have, it's like you throw a little pebble into a pool or into a lake, and these ripples go out and sometimes they intersect and sometimes they don't."

And I responded without even thinking about it, "When that relationship starts and you allow the waves or the ripples to take their natural path, as long as you don't fuck with it, as long as you don't interfere with the natural course of things, which is very difficult, but as long as you allow the universe to unfold, good things happen."

> As hippie as it might sound, it's the fucking truth. The more you allow the universe to play its part, and yourself to be a part of it, the better stuff just happens.

Things continued to break my way. From Simon & Garfunkel, I was back out on the road with Billy, this time for the Innocent Man tour. The album was runner-up for the Record of the Year Grammy,[1] and we did like seventy-five shows in less than nine months. When that wrapped, I was back out on the road with Foreigner for their Agent Provocateur tour. Another smash that took me around the world and paid the bills for the family Sandra and I were starting together.

Even studio gigs were lining up just right. It was September 1985, and I'd been out on the road with Foreigner for like four months, and we happened to be back in New York for gigs in East Rutherford and Madison Square Garden. Lo and behold, Radio Registry gives me a buzz and says "Call James Phelan about a studio gig at the Power Station."

James Phelan was a name I hadn't heard in more than five years. I'd met him only a few times after Trax gigs when the band and I would back his girlfriend. And I remember thinking, "Oh, shit, I hope it's not his girlfriend he wants me to do a session for." She was a mediocre singer, and besides, I was only home for a couple days, spending time with Sandra and the baby, before heading back out on the road for a five-week leg.

But I did return the call, and I'm glad I did. James had gone on to become a producer's rep and his roster included this cat Daniel Lanois (U2, Neil Young, Bob Dylan), who at the time was

---

1. Michael Jackson's *Thriller*, the best-selling record OF ALL TIME, took the honors. Any other year, Billy gets Album of the Year, hands down.

producing Peter Gabriel's *So*.[2] Long story short, I did the gig and that's my saxophone you hear on "Sledgehammer." I just walked into the studio, they played the track, and like with Mutt and Foreigner, what you hear on the radio was my first take. I was back home with Sandra and the baby before dinner. Talk about the stars aligning! I mean, one of the biggest feathers in my career cap— that horn part on that song—was the result of some guy remembering me from a Trax gig five years earlier and Foreigner's tour manager scheduling shows the way he did.

Even Sandra was impressed. Sure, she was miffed when I ducked out on family time, but she also loves Peter Gabriel. And a few months later, we were in the car together and "Sledgehammer" came over the radio, she cranked the volume—not something Sandra does too often—and exclaimed, "I love this song!"[3]

And it's funny, but I remember thinking at that moment, like, "Oh, I got this family thing down."

■ ■ ■

Some gigs are better than others. Some pay well. Some pay like shit. Some come with music material that's so good that, no matter what the pay is, you just can't get enough of it and you're willing to tighten your belt a little for the opportunity to participate. Then there's the high-paying gig where the music blows and you just wanna say, "No, thanks," especially if it's a long tour because playing stuff you're not crazy about night after night, set after set, gets really tough.

---

2. As with Peter's previous two albums, *Melt* and *Security*, the bulk of *So* was recorded at Ashcombe House, Swainswick in Somerset, England.

3. A lot of people agreed with Sandra as "Sledgehammer" reached No. 1 on the *Billboard* and was Peter's biggest hit in North America.

Sandra with Derio, our little "Cumba," in Switzerland. I had the photo laminated to the back of my access badge for the USSR leg of Billy's The Bridge tour. The amazing gig spanned four continents but kept me away from Sandra and the boys for much of 1986 and 1987. (Credit: Rivera Family Collection)

So in 1986 when my good friend Jimmy Rip—yes, the same Jimmy Rip I'd played with at Trax in the late '70s—called to say, "Yoko Ono is going out on a world tour and I'm putting the band together," you might think I passed. After all, I'd just been on this amazing five-year run.

And now what? *Yoko Ono?* I think everyone can agree, including the performance artist herself, Yoko's approach to music, which has been classified as "avant-garde" and "noise," isn't exactly *let your hair down* rock 'n' roll. She'd prefer to jar a person, forcing them to second-guess melody and harmony rather than keep them smiling and snapping along or rocking out. She's not a musician in the typical sense, or for that matter, a person who's either willing or able to sing on key. Not that there's anything wrong with exploring discordance—it's not everyone's cup of tea, including mine.

But here's the thing: I did take the gig and I was more than grateful to have it. Why? First off, I didn't have to audition. And that felt pretty good because I was becoming a known commodity: *Oh, sure, I know Mark Rivera. He plays with everyone.* Artists were no longer asking if I was any good; now they were only asking if I was available. And that's the second reason I took the gig: I was available. Because after the Agent Provocateur tour wrapped, things went suddenly quiet.

Everyone thinks you've got gigs lined up, when the truth is maybe you do, maybe you don't. And if you don't have something lined up, you're not about to go out and broadcast to others, "Hey, I'm not gigging, ladies and gentlemen." Because then they might start thinking you're not such hot shit anymore. Like any other commodity, people want you more when they think they can't get you, and they want you less when they know they can. Any whiff of desperation on your part just leaves a residue. So maybe those people who thought you were the cat's pajamas ten minutes ago, now start asking questions you don't want them to ask, like, "Why's this guy not gigging all of the sudden? Is there something wrong with him? Maybe he's too big for his britches and becoming a drag out on the road. Is he hitting the sauce too hard, snorting too much of that white powder? Yikes, maybe we should contact someone else . . ."

So, the phone wasn't ringing, and I didn't know how to make it start. It's like one of those movies about a ship out at sea, and there's always the scene where the wind's gone slack and the boat is stuck out in the middle of the ocean and the crew is sweating bullets and the sun is beating down and everyone is waiting for the wind to pick back up. Well, that's what it was like after we wrapped that Foreigner tour. I was back home for a month. No wind. Two months. No wind. Three months . . . Where's the fucking wind?!

You might say, "What's the big deal, Mark? It's only a few months." Yeah, but this was the first time in five years that I hadn't jumped right into something else and all that time I'd been spending money I didn't have. I mean, I'd come in from the road after being gone for weeks at a time, and I'd always want to walk in the door like Santa Claus. Fancy clothes, jewelry, toys. Anything I saw, I bought. Shit, I bought more than ten thousand dollars' worth of recording equipment—Yamaha keyboards, Fostex reel-to-reel machines, speakers, and microphones—to set up a little recording studio in the new house's basement. Why? Because I was a rock star and that's what rock stars like Mick and Lou did. And just like paying for the house, I was somehow under this delusion that I could afford it.

And it's okay to go spending all your dough when it's just yourself. But when you have a family and a mortgage and all of that, it becomes a serious problem. It's not like you can go missing mortgage payments.

And if I didn't understand what owning a house meant when I had my brilliant idea of, "Let's get out of the city and raise our family in a house upstate," I certainly did once we moved into the new place. We weren't in the house for a month when Sandra, who notices everything, says, "There's something wrong with the toilet. It's getting a lot of silt or something."

And I'm like, "Ah, you're super paranoid."

But, of course, our well pump blows. We're talking thousands of dollars to replace it, and I didn't have the money.

Again, I'm here doing this whole new thing, and I'm obviously not very good at it. Doing the hustle, bouncing around the city, finding another gig—okay, it took me a decade, but now I'm good at that shit. But this family stuff, I'm in way over my head. Because I'm a dad. I'm no longer a musician who just wrapped a tour and is awaiting a next one. I'm a musician who is out of work. Period. Because now I own a home. And I just bought a car. And all this shit on my plate. *And now my fucking well pump dies?*

So the guy comes to the house, and obviously he's looking at a husband, wife, and their son and they need water. He replaces our well pump before telling me how much it's gonna cost. Then he comes inside, and he says, "Has there been any lightning in the last week or so?"

And I looked at him and I could tell he was trying to tell me something, like *think before you answer this, asshole.* So I said, "What's the right answer?"

He goes, "There was, right?"

I said, "Yes, there was."

And then he said, "Well, I wouldn't worry about it, Mr. Rivera. Your insurance probably covers lightning strikes."

I looked at Sandra and said, "We have insurance, right?"

She nodded.

And the plumber, whose name was John Finley, said, "Sure you do, Mr. Rivera. The bank won't give you the loan on the house without the insurance."

"Oh yeah," I replied.

So John Finley, who I still remember in my prayers, put it in his report as a lightning strike, which was covered by insurance. And he did all of the repair and replacement work and didn't ask for a dollar until my insurance money came.

Anyway, the point is that now I got a family. Now I got a house. And the idea of not working for a few months has serious repercussions. I'd wake up in the middle of the night fretting the money that wasn't coming in, fretting the money that I'd spent so frivolously only a few months previously, and I'd head down to the basement to the music room, where I'd just stare at all of this equipment that I'd purchased and think, "Goddamit, I wish I didn't do that." Because instead of a creative space, it became a cage.

I'd go down to the studio, thinking, "Okay, I'll write my way out of this." But the songs wouldn't come, and all I was left with was staring at this stupid synthesizer, wishing it had never come into my house. I mean, all of the recording gear was like six months' worth of mortgage payments.

I could only blame myself. No one forced me to buy that stuff or anything else. Sandra certainly never said she needed the jewelry or the pearls or the clothing. She never made me feel like, *Oh, I need these new shoes.* And what really would have made us happier was less stress in the house. And all I'd done was increase the stress, like, *There goes Daddy, stressing out about money again.*

So, yeah, I was thrilled and proud of how much I was accomplishing with my career, but as a husband and father, I wasn't getting it done. I'd made the mistake of thinking, *Hey, this is never going to end.* When you're doing really well and tens of thousands of people are loving what you do, you think you're gonna walk on water next. And you make good money—you make $2,000 a week for a while and you think it's never gonna change or it's never gonna end, but it does. And when it does, it's like, *Now what do I do?* And suddenly the walls feel like they're caving in.

So, I'd go out on these long walks in the woods around our house, trying to gain some perspective, but I'd always wind up imagining that, only a couple hundred years earlier, Native Americans would be out there hunting, living off the land, totally capable, and that if it was left to me to hunt for my family, we'd starve. It brought me down even further to think there are people who can provide everything, no matter the hardship. Not even the monetary aspect of it, but just *I'll build a house if I have to. I'll make a fire.*

I'll keep us warm. Being out in the woods made me feel totally vulnerable, and I'd walk back into the house thinking, *Great, you've got this great life going, but you have no idea how to keep it going. You're fucking useless.*

I even started pulling hours with my neighbor's landscaping company. I saw him one day at the end of the driveway. He was riding by and stopped to say hello, and he knew I was sweating my next gig and said, "If you ever want to get some physical work in, come join me." Or something like that.

I said, "Are you serious?" In other words, *You'd let me do some work?*

And I explained I didn't know how to run the machines, but he said, "No, just the grunt work."

So that's what I did. Cutting down trees and stacking and hauling wood, pulling stumps, trenching. It was incredibly physical. We'd start at the crack of ugly and go all day. I think he paid me a hundred bucks a day. Cash. And though I was half-embarrassed that I had to do it, I remember being in incredible shape and finally sleeping very well. It'd be nine o'clock at night and I'd be out cold. Half the time, I'd be asleep before the baby, exhausted from the work and content with myself that I wasn't above doing it. That's something that my father would always say to never allow into your mind. He'd say, "A plate of food is a plate of food." When you have a family, as long as you're not hurting anybody, you do what you need to do. And at that moment, for me, it was landscaping.

Still, it wasn't paying my mortgage, and at one point, I had to drive to Brooklyn to ask my dad for help. We all drove down together—Sandra, the baby and me. We arrived and Sandra took the baby upstairs to my sister's apartment where our two nephews were. And my mom drifted upstairs with them to be with all the grandkids.

My father and I were alone in the living room. I can picture him sitting in his rocking chair. Above him is his favorite picture, taken a few years earlier, and it shows my father and me shaking hands and the Foreigner *4* record on the wall. He's so proud of me.

I mean, here's my dad, a union guy. He worked for RCA Communications for like thirty-five years and he'd saved up all this money. And he took the money and put it into some CDs or something. At first people said, "Oh, you should've done this or that." And lo and behold, when the stock market plummeted, he had guarantees of like 7 percent on the CDs. He was like the smartest guy on the block, and now his son—Mr. Rock 'n' Roll big shot— was broke and needed to borrow money.

So I'm looking at him sitting beneath that picture, and I don't think I cried yet, but I was close to it. And my father was very perceptive. He knew something was up and he just smiled and gently asked, "What's going on? Everything all right?"

I said, "Actually, no, Dad. Things are basically far from all right." And I explained the jam I was in.

And the only question he asked was, "What do you need?"

It wasn't: *Oh, this is gonna cost . . . And when do I get it back?* He said, "What do you need? That's my gift to you."

Then I broke down, sobbing because I was so thankful and so dismayed that I had to ask and he said, "Let's take care of this before your mother comes down." I'm sure my mother found out eventually, but he didn't want her to know that day that I was in such desperation.

A few weeks later, Jimmy Rip called me up about Yoko. So, you bet your ass I was happy for the gig. Like James Phelan calling about the Peter Gabriel gig, and John Finley the plumber saving my ass, the universe was looking out for me, and all I could say was, "Thank you."

24

OUT WITH THE BOYS

When my mom got very sick, we were playing between New York and Philadelphia. It was with Billy and Elton John, the Face to Face tour, and we had a bunch of shows in the area. So, I went to see her, and I sat with her in her living room. My father had passed eleven years before and I could see in her face she was a little teary. And I held her hand. I said, "Mom. What's wrong? Are you in pain?"

She goes, "I don't feel the pain anymore."

I said, "Are you scared?"

"Scared of what? Dying? No! Not at all."

I said, "Why are you upset?"

And she starts to break down and says, "I don't want to be a burden on you. I don't want you to ever miss a show because of me."

"Mom—"

She stopped me. She said, "Mark, promise me that you'll never miss a show. No matter what happens you'll always do the show. Promise me."

I said, "Okay."

It was a way for her to put herself to rest, for her own peace, so she wouldn't feel like that on her last breath that, *Oh, no. Now he's got to stay home.*

She passed away about a week later, in the morning, and I got to hold her hand. That evening we had a show. It was tough but I played the show. There was one point I looked over at Billy. I looked at Liberty. And at one point each of them would look at me, almost with a kiss, and then look up at the sky. Yep, she's there. She's here. She's watching me.

And the day that we buried her—two or three days later—we had another show and I played that one, too.

Mom understood the most important rule of all in this business: always be gigging. Sandra and our sons do, too. Over the years they've borne the brunt. Sure, I can say that I've provided a good life for my family. There was always a nice house and food on the table. But I also missed a lot of stuff. Weddings, funerals, the big game . . .

But all that said, there are some silver linings to having a dad who's in rock 'n' roll.

I was touring the Northeast with Daryl Hall and John Oates, and my oldest son, Derio, was five years old. The tour manager, Brian Doyle, who was crazy about Derio, said, "Why don't we take him out on the road with us for a couple days?" Brian's a great guy. He now owns the Paramount on Long Island and is a very dear friend.

"Do you think that would be okay?" I asked, thrilled at the prospect of spending a little extra time with my son.

"Sure," he said. "I'll look after him when you're on stage."

So just like that, Derio joined us for a few dates.

We'd hang out all day, father and son, and he'd take naps on the bus or in the dressing room, and right before the show I'd tuck him in his tiny bed we'd set up on the dressing room couch, and

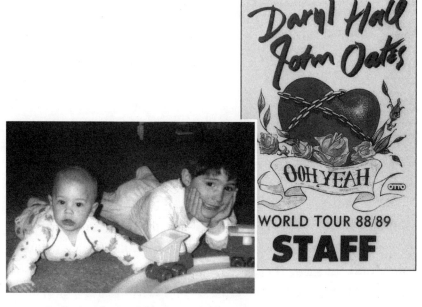

A photograph of Derio and his new baby brother, Moreo, laminated to the backside of my access badge for the OOH YEAH World Tour. (Credit: Rivera Family Collection)

Brian would watch him while the band played. Then, around midnight, the bus would be ready to take us to the next place, and I'd gently pick Derio up from the couch and move him into my bunk on the bus. That was the drill.

Now, there were two lounges on the bus, one in the front, the other in the back. The bunks were in between. And Daryl Hall used to sleep in the front lounge. It was understood, that's where Daryl slept. Everyone else took a bunk.

So, one night, it's about three o'clock in the morning and everyone's sleeping. Everyone except for Derio, who had woken up and crept out of the bunk. He wanted to explore. So he walked to the front of the bus, scooting past Daryl and up to the bus driver. And the bus driver was driving the bus and couldn't exactly stop or call out to someone to come take this kid, so he said, "Heya, kid. You can sit here," pointing to the passenger seat, "but you got to put the seatbelt on."

Derio, who was a pretty easygoing kid, said, "Okay," and sat down and, I'm sure after some dexterous coaching from the bus driver, strapped in. He was content, staring out the window, so high above the road, checking out the other cars and the head-lights and whatever parts of civilization were still aglow. Then, sometime around 4 AM, he was off again, and the bus driver says, "Okay, now you have to go back to Daddy in the bunk."

So, Derio heads back. Only this time he stops next to Daryl Hall sleeping on the couch. I mean he's like full-on sleeping—the dude had just worked his ass off for three hours, belting out soulful tunes, radio hits that the crowd never seemed to get enough of. So, he was probably pretty tired and was now sleeping like a baby when Derio, for some reason, opened his eyelids. He just pressed his five-year-old fingers into the guy's eyes and pulled back the curtains.

"Hello!"

Of course, Daryl, who as it turned out wasn't really into kids, screamed bloody murder.

I woke up and realized my son wasn't with me. So I shot out of bed and Daryl was like, "He tried to open my fucking eyes, man!"

He obviously didn't gravitate toward kids and was repelled as far away from this one as possible, pointing an incredulous finger at the little monster. Not that I could blame Daryl; small kids on headline tour buses weren't exactly your typical hazard. Drugs, booze, upset girlfriends: these were more typical than an eyelid-peeling five-year-old.

So, I put on a front for Daryl. "Oh, yeah, I'll take care of this. Don't you worry, he won't do it again." And I took Derio back to the bunks with me.

"Did I do something wrong?" Derio asked as we got back into the bed.

"Nah," I told him. "Mr. Daryl is just new to the whole kid thing."

And he took it like, "Okay." I never had to say, "Don't do it again."

So Daryl wasn't a big fan of the experiment, but the tour manager, Brian, thought it was hilarious, and sometime after that he got married and started a family. He has a couple kids of his own now. He and his wife are still together and they're doing well. So, I think sometimes you see how a fellow road warrior is able to have a family, and you gain confidence. They simply say, "Hey, I can do that."

As the boys got older, I'd always tell Sandra that I'd like to take the boys out on tour, and she'd say, "I don't know." But finally, she relented, and I took the two lads out. It was 1995 when I was out with Ringo for the first time. The kids and I flew into St. Louis and stayed in a Four Seasons Hotel.

I remember Derio, who was now eleven years old, walking into the hotel right behind me, taking cues from how I behaved and who I spoke to. If I said "Thank you" or "Hello" or "Have a nice day," Derio would say it, too. I'd shake hands, he'd shake hands. It was like he, the older boy, wanted me to know that he understood this was a big deal and was old enough to behave responsibly. So, he wouldn't fight with his younger brother over who got to push the elevator button—just tell him which button to push. He wouldn't need to be the one to put the room key into the hotel door—again, his little brother could have that bit of fun—so long as he, Derio, got to keep the key in his pocket. Again, he wanted to show his dad he was responsible.

His younger brother, Moreo, was a different story. I remember the first time we went into the hotel room, he walked into the room and hopped up on the bed and grabbed the TV remote. I must have gone to the bathroom for a second and washed my hands or whatever. But when I came out, Moreo was flipping through the channels, munching on a pack of M&Ms and a bag of potato chips, and sipping on a Coca-Cola. Seven years old and he's kicking back on this big giant bed and says, "Dad, this is hotel living."

And I said, "I'm glad you like it, son, because you just cost me forty bucks."

I laughed, of course. I was delighted to see my boys. Delighted to check in on where they were in life, getting snapshots into their personalities as they were and what they might become. They were good boys, and while it's sad that I didn't see the kids every day, I was afforded certain opportunities because there are advantages to being a road-musician family man. When you're home, you're really home. And when you're on the road, sometimes you can afford to take the kids with you. And the idea of being Mr. Mom out on the road as a rock star is hilarious. Those are not two worlds that converge in people's minds. But it happens.

25

SIDEMAN REQUIRED

■ **Brewster, New York, 2020**

I look around my bedroom and there's like forty small boxes full of saxophone reeds, tucked here and there. They're different strengths and stuff and they're all over the place. This whole house is swimming in gear. I mean, if I looked under the bed right now, I'd see four guitars, two flutes, an alto saxophone, a bari, and my oldest soprano sax. The Fender Telecaster is over on the stand and a flute is on the bed because I was practicing this morning.

Everything is oiled, ready to go. (Well, almost everything—one of my tenors needs some love.) Because a sideman never knows when the next call is coming. But when it does, he'd better be ready.

And when the call comes, you start pulling out the gear, practicing the songs, writing out the lyrics, figuring out what instrument you might use on what song. Maybe you have a month to prepare, maybe it's just a few days. Again, you'd better be ready. Because the guys from Rock-It Cargo—the freight and logistics company that everyone and their brother in the entertainment

SIDEMAN

industry uses to move their shit—are coming by the house to pick up your road case. "Big Rico 50." That's what's printed on my road case, which is about the size of a refrigerator and weighs about three hundred pounds loaded. After a tour, the guys from Rock-It bring it to the house and it lives out in the garage, next to the tools and the winter tires. But the guys are coming back for it again, so the gear comes out of the house and gets loaded in the case.

The first thing to go in is the bari sax because we have to make sure there's enough room. Then the two tenors, the alto, the soprano, the flute. Then a Telecaster or Stratocaster, and a Takamine acoustic electric. Finally, my "bag of noise," which is all my percussion gear. Congas, maracas, claves, tambourines, shakers, a triangle . . . it all goes in the case, and the guys from Rock-It take it away.

And then, maybe you've got a couple days before you're back out on the road. You spend time with the family, and you practice on instruments you still have around the house. (There's never a shortage.) Or maybe you held on to one of the instruments for the road just for some extra practice on a song you've never played in that register or on that instrument and you want to have it fresh in your head and in your fingers when you arrive at rehearsal. Because, again, the sideman better be ready to go.

■ June 1995

It started with a phone call from George Travis. George is a production manager, putting entire crews together for big shows. Madonna, Bruce, AC/DC, Shania Twain . . . they'd all call George Travis when they wanted to put a show on the road. The same way I had a Rolodex of musician friends that I could call, George had a Rolodex of technical people, from front-of-house sound guys to guitar and drum techs backstage. That's his gig.

198

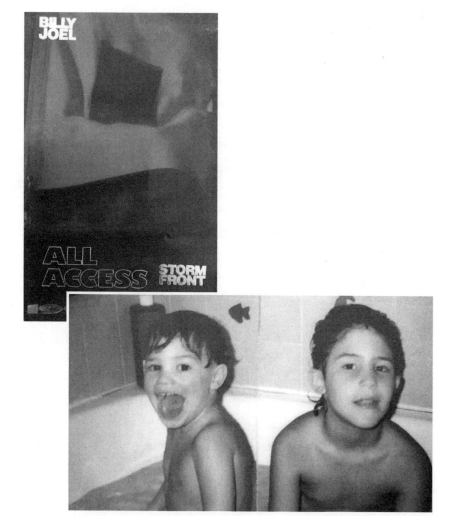

Growing boys: Moreo with his big brother, Derio.
Sometimes I'm far away but my family is always close
to my heart. (Credit: Rivera Family Collection)

George and I are pretty tight. We've been working together
since the Foreigner *4* days. I remember back in the '80s, we were
in Hawaii—or somewhere else with a nice beach—touring with
Billy. Sandra was visiting, and George's wife came out with their

kids—twin boys who were toddlers at the time. And I told George, "Hey, why don't you and Lenore go out tonight. Let Sandra and me watch the kids."

"Well, that's really nice of you to offer," George said. "But Lenore hasn't left them alone with anyone yet. I'd hate for you and Sandra to get stuck with the trial run."

I said, "George. I'm your guy. Go out and let us watch the kids."

So they did, and he and Lenore had a great time. And it was good for Sandra and me because she was pregnant with Derio. We got to practice playing Mom and Dad for a few hours. I've still got a picture that Sandra took of the babies laying on my belly, *finally* asleep.

So, anyway, we're both family guys, and it's not unusual for either one of us to pick up the phone and call the other just to check in.

Then George said, "I don't know if you heard this, but Ringo's putting together a tour."

"Yeah," I said. "I wish I could be on it."

I knew that the former Beatles drummer was putting together a tour with another All Starr Band, which he started to roll out in the late '80s as an opportunity for former rock 'n' roll chart-toppers to share a stage with each other and play some serious sets in some serious venues. But I also knew there was no chance of me hooking up with the act because the band was already slated to include Clarence Clemons, the larger-than-life saxophone player from the E Street Band.

But then George said, "It turns out that Clarence can't make it work. Do you have an interest?"

And my heart skipped a beat because it couldn't have come at a better time . . .

Imagine this. It's 1995. And here I am, again. Another lull and I didn't save enough money. Even if I save enough for half a year—from the time Billy and Elton's Face to Face tour ended until I started working with Ringo—this time it was like this long period, about three years. I even went and got my Series 6 to sell life insurance, which I hated.

What had happened was my friend Paul, who's a great guy and handles all of my insurance, knew I was struggling and said, "Why don't you come work with me? You'd be great. The people will love you and we can close these big deals. We'll get key-man insurance at all these big companies and any one of these premiums could make you $50 to $100,000 over the first year."

And I'm like, "Yeah, sounds great. I could do it."

So, I spent weeks studying to take the test, which I passed. I bought the shirts, I put on jackets, I did the whole thing.

And I'd go to some guy's house and he and his wife are there talking, and we're talking and I'm leading on and there'd be drinks and hors d'oeuvres and shit. The people would roll out the red car-pet. They'd ask me about playing gigs and what's this person like and that person, and it was all just a bunch of bullshit. Yeah, they brought out the wine, but they wouldn't close the deal. I went to scores of people's homes. They'd all send me their friends' numbers and we'd line something up, but all anyone did was ask me questions about Christie Brinkley. *What's it like doing this? What's it like doing that?* And we didn't close one fucking deal the whole time. It was almost like, it was nice having you over, want to have a drink? Want to meet my friend? And I'm like, *I don't want to meet your friend. I don't even want to be here talking to you, but are you gonna sign the piece of paper?* Nothing ever closed. So that was another dead end.

But people thought, *Oh, he's Billy Joel's sax player, so he's got to be okay.*

Fortunately, things changed. And as usual, it was a phone call.

Like all phone calls that potentially land a gig, the moment someone like George asks you, "Do you have an interest?" is the exact moment when it becomes very real. It crystallizes in your head and you see yourself up on stage alongside the rest of the act. Sometimes the image is great and sometimes the image is like, *eh*. This time, the image was almost too good to be true. *Ringo Starr? A Beatle? Holy shit!*

So, I calmed myself down and probably said something mature like, "Oh, fuck yeah!"

"Good," George said. "Clarence bailed in the eleventh hour so Ringo's not hot on saxophone players right now, but I put your name in the hat. And Ringo said he's willing to give you a shot."

■ ■ ■

There had been two previous All Starr Bands, the first in 1989 and the second in 1992. Ringo's idea was to bring together a live supergroup composed of various artists performing each other's songs. So in 1989, for example, the band featured Joe Walsh of the Eagles (guitar and vocals), Nils Lofgren of Crazy Horse and the E Street Band (guitar, accordion, and vocals), Dr. John (piano, bass, vocals), Billy Preston (keyboards and vocals), Rick Danko (bass, guitar, vocals), and Levon Helm (drums, harmonica, vocals) of the Band, Clarence Clemons of the E Street Band (saxophone, tambourine, percussion, vocals), and of course, Ringo Starr (drums, percussion, and vocals). That's a lot of star talent with a lot of chart-topping material for audiences to sink their teeth into.

Now Ringo was planning to go out on the road again with a new cast, and it suddenly seemed like I might have a spot.

And while I was beyond ecstatic, some anxiety stirred in my gut. Because I wasn't a star. I was a sideman. Sure, previous All Starr Bands had included sidemen to help round out the sound, but I was replacing Clarence Clemons, whose celebrity status took him out of the realm of sidemen and firmly planted him in the "star" category. So much so that when Clarence, a.k.a. The Big Man, a

6'8" former defensive lineman, was part of the All Starrs, the sets would include "Pink Cadillac" and "Glory Days." Because audiences would see the big guy, who looked like a giant tree next to all these tiny musicians, and say, "Oh, that's Clarence Clemons from the E Street Band." His physical presence and big sound were arguably as much a part of those songs' identity as Bruce himself, and such currency gave Clarence a seat at the All Starr table as a *feature*, not a sideman.

I, however, wasn't a household name who could sell tickets. Assuming Ringo liked me at rehearsals and I made the band, we wouldn't be showcasing any songs from my repertoire on stage. So, no Billy or Hall & Oates or Foreigner or anything else. And if I was going to be of any value to Ringo's band, it was purely going to be as a sideman, and I needed to walk into those rehearsals prepared to contribute whatever was required on whatever instrument to help the set sound fucking amazing. And, now, making my way around the house, gathering my gear and thinking about what instruments I wanted to bring, that is exactly what I was determined to do. I *wanted* this gig.

But I had to move fast. Rehearsals were less than a week away.

■ ■ ■

I arrived in Vancouver the day before rehearsals, and the only person I saw from the band was the drummer, Zak Starkey, who besides being in the current lineup for the Who and one of the best drummers in the world, is also Ringo's son. Anyway, he was coming out of his hotel room when I was coming in and we just chatted for a moment. I was like, "It's nice to meet you," and I remember smelling herb outside of Zak's door and thinking, "I got to look into this," because we were in Canada and it was always a little bit more of a difficult proposition scoring weed across the border.

And the thing is, I didn't know *anyone* from the band I was, hopefully, about to join. The last time that was true for me was before 1980. Foreigner, Billy, Simon & Garfunkel, Hall & Oates—there was always someone in the group who I'd worked with already. But this time I was going in without a wingman. That may sound kind of silly. After all, by 1995, I was a seasoned vet, playing on stage with music's best and in front of stadium-sized crowds for the past fifteen years. When you add it up, that's like millions of people. But sometimes playing for large crowds is less nerve-racking than intimate situations. Especially if those intimate situations involve people you've never played with and, more importantly, grew up idolizing. And Ringo Starr and the group he'd assembled for his third All Starr Band was like a *who's who* list of my childhood heroes. Here's who we had:

Ringo Starr (the Beatles): drums, vocals
Randy Bachman (Bachman–Turner Overdrive and the Guess Who): guitar, vocals
Mark Farner (Grand Funk Railroad): guitar, harmonica, vocals
Felix Cavaliere (the Rascals): organ, keyboards, percussion, vocals
John Entwistle (the Who): bass, vocals
Billy Preston: keyboards, vocals
Zak Starkey (the Who): drums

Take Felix Cavaliere, founder and front man of the Rascals, for example. It's like, *Are you kidding me? I get the chance to be up onstage with that guy?* I'd been spinning Rascals records since I was fourteen. Along with the Righteous Brothers, they were the kings of blue-eyed soul. As a kid, I'd listen to them on my father's stereo or in my little basement den and pick up the guitar or sit down at the piano and teach myself the chord changes. Then I'd show them to the guys in Maitrex Square and we'd practice, sometimes ad nauseum, in the basement beneath the Chinese laundromat before performing them for the high school make-out parties and Battles of the Bands. When I got older, I still played Rascals classics in clubs and dive bars. Even today, whenever Billy does a sound-check, half the time we just break into the stuff we grew up on. So "Good Lovin'" or "Groovin'" or "People Got to Be Free." They're always fair game. Again, they're classics.

So, walking into a room with all of these legends and not having that wingman for support—a Bobby Mayo or a T-Bone Wolk or a David Brown pulling for me—was a big challenge. Would I live up to it? Could I, a mere mortal, enter the Hall of the Gods and find favor? Or would they find me wanting—my performance too tentative in the big moment—and cast me out on my ass?

The following day, I got to rehearsal, which was at this big theater in Vancouver because the stage was large enough to run the technical aspects for sound and lighting. And George Travis introduced me to Ringo, who could not have been more gracious. If he held any grudges against sax players after being burned by Clarence Clemons, he didn't show it. He was the second Beatle I'd ever met, and like John, was completely cordial. And then I got to meet Billy Preston, which was like, *holy fuck,* because here was a guy who was only one of five musicians ever credited on a Beatles' recording, and who John Lennon had actually proposed should join the Fab Four as its fifth member. That's how talented the dude was. And then of course, there's John Entwistle, who I'd only seen in concert when I'd seen the Who, one of the biggest and most iconic bands of all time. It was like, *Whoa! Where am I right now?* Because I was starstruck. And yeah, I remembered what my mother always told me—*treat those who are famous like they're not, those who are not like they are*—and I was probably doing a decent job of that. But still, on the inside at least, I was in total awe, like I was fourteen all over again.

So then Ringo goes, "Shall we start?"

And now we're up on stage and it's all about to start happening when I suddenly realize something extraordinary: *I was totally calm.* It was a sense of, "I want to shine, I want to be able to participate on this level." And as mind-blowing as the moment was—*I can't believe I'm about to be playing music with these guys*—I was very comfortable. Which is a weird place. You would think your palms might be sweaty or your mouth dry and you wouldn't be able to sing a note. But as the first song was being counted in, somehow in my heart of hearts I knew I was ready for whatever was about to happen. Like I'd waited my whole life to be in this band.

26

HALL OF THE GODS

■ My birthday is tomorrow. Sixty-eight . . .

The idea of rockers becoming old men is strange, even to me. Because it's true, rock 'n' roll is a young man's sport. I remember a story George Travis told me. It was a few years before I became involved in the All Starrs. We were in Boston, I think, and I asked George what the first All Starr tour was like, being around all of those legends, and of course he had wonderful things to say. But he told me something that caught me by surprise.

"They take a lot of naps," George said.

"What do you mean, *naps*?" I asked.

And George, who was the tour manager, said that they'd have all these cots laid out backstage because a bunch of older guys— Dr. John, Levon Helm, Jim Keltner (Traveling Wilburys, Eric Clapton, Bob Dylan)—would be wiped out and they all just wanted to catch some Z's before a show.

"Yeah," he said, "they'd be doing four or maybe five shows a week, flying all over the world. And for some of the guys it was like, 'Whoa,' because it had been a long time since they'd done anything like that. So, instead of a backroom party setup with the hippie lights and booze and stuff, we'd put out the cots so the guys could have naptime."

And that blew my mind. It was around 1990, so I was still a couple years from forty, and it was the first time that I really remember thinking,"Oh, I guess rockers get older, too." As a kid, it would have been impossible to imagine your heroes, the guys on the records with the awesome hairdos and killer clothes, ever becoming old men. Many of them, of course, never would because they died young. But rockers getting older just doesn't compute in most people's brains, even for the artists themselves. It's sorta like, "Huh?" Like when I turn on the radio and it's a "classic" rock station, and I laugh because it feels like only yesterday when I was running to the record store to buy the latest Hendrix or whatever.

Carole King once said, "Songs are like pancakes. The first pass you have, the griddle isn't hot enough and maybe you need to change your ingredients up a bit. But by the third or fourth pancake, when the griddle is just right and it's oiled up, that's when everything comes about."

Yeah, the first pancake is always for the dog. Unless you're a front man like Billy Joel or a sideman like Bobby Mayo, both of whom I consider to be the elite when it comes to performance chops and pretty much nail everything the first time, even the most practiced musicians need a few passes to really lock a new number down. But from up on my riser, it was apparent that getting the mix right for the All Starr Band was going to be different. Again, an All Starr Band is not a cover band where members can jump right in. Instead, it's guys who each have been wildly successful over many decades, and as a result of exclusively playing the same material, have grown a bit calcified. And that's tough because now they needed to get back some of their dexterity and be a little more like sidemen, like well-oiled Swiss Army knives. I mean, look at the various types of music in that third All Starr Band: Grand Funk Railroad, the Who, Bachman–Turner Overdrive, the Rascals, and the Beatles. Five different styles of music to take on.

Our first song was Ringo's "It Don't Come Easy." It's the perfect opener. Everyone's coming in on the one, including me on tenor saxophone, for eight measures and weaving the song's hook and basic changes around a series of drum rolls. From there the song goes straight into the first chorus. That's a lot of energy and is a good way to immediately see what's what.

And that's the beauty of the sideman's perspective. From my riser, away from the center of things, I could see how each musician was reacting to the performance and to one another. It's like when you look at a painting on the wall. Sometimes when you look at a picture straight on and up close, you only see so much. You gotta move around the room, look from a distance. From there, you can take a real assessment of the whole thing.

So, what was my assessment of the All Starr Band as we made our way through this first leg? Well, to be honest, we kind of sucked. Sure, there was energy. But it was unfocused, undirected, sloppy. It was apparent that not everyone knew the exact chords—there were minor thirds where there should be majors or suspensions or vice versa. And when we hit the chorus, the tight three-part harmony that's supposed to be supporting Ringo's vocal was more like a free for all.

It wasn't all bad. Starkey on drums and Entwistle on bass were locked in. You could tell right away that the Who's drummer and bass player had been working together for a long time. And Billy Preston, who along with Zak and Ringo was the only returning member of the band, was playing this amazing *diggadee diggadee diggadee* on the keys, but you really couldn't hear him because the guitars were crowding in, giving him no space.

Obviously, not all of these guys had practiced as much as they should have and didn't know the basic organization of the song. They didn't know the roadmap. *It goes back to the intro after the second episode at the solo, it goes back into the sax solo, it goes back and now it goes back to the bridge.* Even worse, they were breaking one of musical performance's golden rules: "When in doubt, lay out." That's standard operating procedure: if you don't know what you're supposed to play in a particular point or pass, lay out—play nothing—because a sonic hole is better than too much noise or, even worse, the missed note.

So I was a little shocked that the band wasn't as prepared as I thought it would be. But then it hit me: *Of course these guys don't know what to do. They aren't used to playing other people's songs.* And it's funny because there I was, stressing out the past week to make sure that I was locked and loaded, when the big concern wasn't what *I* could do. I mean, I'd been playing "covers" my whole career. As a sideman, that's my job! Even if I hadn't prepared a single thing, I certainly wasn't going to cock up the sound. But these guys—particularly Randy Bachman, Mark Farner, and Felix Cavaliere—had spent their careers playing their own material. Only now they were essentially being asked to be a cover band.

After the rough start, I'm thinking someone's going to say something like, "Okay, guys, not bad. Now let's try to figure out what's what," and then offer a prescription on the various parts. But nobody says anything. It was almost like everyone was too embarrassed to ask, "How was that?" Even Felix Cavaliere, who Ringo had appointed as musical director, was just sort of fiddling with his keyboard.

So now I was really like, *what the fuck?* Because I wanted to say something, to offer a suggestion. But I was just the sideman here for a tryout! It's not like I could say, "Hey, guys, that sucked and here's what we should do." But I couldn't bite my tongue, either. Because good, better, indifferent—I usually speak my mind.

It's like the horn parts with Paul Simon: *Well, to tell you the truth, Paul, I think the horn parts are pretty lame.* And it's never an ego thing. It's simply a matter of getting the song right. If a part could be better, I'll say it. If a chord is wrong, I'll say it. If somebody's singing a major third instead of a minor third, I'll say it. It's like my good friend Jimmy Bralower preaches: "You know, you're in a room and all of a sudden the guy thinks he knows what's going on. And somebody's gotta say *that's not how it goes.*"

Because I loved the songs and had such huge respect for these guys Ringo had assembled. I wanted to see them at their best. From the guitar lines to the bass parts to the drums to the horns to the backup harmonies, I understood every measure. Sure, there were a few that I hadn't played a ton or I needed to know on a different instrument. But I'd just spent the last week practicing. My ears and hands had been soaking this stuff up. Because that's what a sideman does. Playing all sorts of instruments on all sorts of songs and knowing what everyone else is playing is what I do. So I had to step up.

I leaned into my microphone and said, "Hey, guys, that was fun. Before we do another pass, could we run a chorus a capella? I just want to make sure I'm singing the right part."

Now, why would I say it that way? I mean, of course I know the part *I* am singing. But, again, I couldn't up and call these guys out and say something like, *"Let's run through a chorus without the instruments because you guys don't know your ass from your elbow and we need to clear the deck and start all over with just the voices."* Instead, I made a suggestion and posed an uncertainty on *my* part as its impetus: *It's not you guys. It's me. I gotta learn this—could you help me out?* In taking the self-effacing approach, I didn't step on any toes. Because even the coolest musicians can get a bit hot, *especially* if the suggestion might be construed as questioning their musical abilities. And each of these guys was used to calling the shots, not being called out, so the potential for touching a nerve was pretty big.

Fortunately, the approach worked. Everyone was like, *Oh, good idea. Let's help the sideman out.* And with the process started, I had my foot in the door. Because you clear out the instruments and everyone hears who's singing what. Things become cleaner and you can make further suggestions on how to tidy up. So, if it's a three-part chorus and there's five guys singing, you can say, "*Hey, if we thin this out, it'll sound more like the record.*" And again, they go along with it, and now you can really get your hands dirty and start assigning parts.

And that's what I did. I said to Mark Farner, who has that wonderful upper register, "You take the high part and I'll take the part below that." And then we had Billy Preston doubling Ringo on the main vocal. *Ahh, that's better!*

Now we were cooking with gas. Limiting the vocals allowed the other players to concentrate exclusively on their instruments. So, Randy Bachman could concentrate on the crucial rhythm guitar part, and anytime you tell a guitar player, *You don't have to sing in this one*, it gives him the freedom to do what he's got to do. Because somebody's got to be carrying that *cha-ching cha-ching.* That's vital. And Felix Cavaliere, who tended to play big organ parts, could focus on his harmony and play a little less, which afforded Billy Preston's keyboard more space in the sound. And once those assignments went out and we cleared up a couple of the chord changes, we played through the song a few more times and started to lock things down. Then we moved on to the next few songs.

By the fifth song, I could see that all of the guys were appreciative. They understood we needed someone to direct and put each member in spots where he could ultimately succeed. And the problem was that Felix, as the musical director, really wasn't up for the challenge. At least not in this band, where the need for a more hands-on approach was apparent after the first batch of songs. I think he thought it would be easy; he would just have one of the techs play the CD over the speakers and then everybody would hear what they needed to hear and figure it out. He didn't have it in him to explain to people what had to be done. It's one of the hardest things in music—to break things down, note by note, section by section, and tell somebody how it goes. And it's not where Felix shined.

And remember, these guys were motivated to put on a great show. Because times had certainly changed since the '60s and the '70s when, for example, Grand Funk Railroad sold out Shea Stadium almost as quickly as the Beatles did. And now, with the exception of Entwistle and Starkey with the Who, none of these guys could sell enough tickets to fill the large venues Ringo booked for the All Starrs. *But together as five legends in one show?* That was a big ticket, and Ringo was giving each of them the chance to once again showcase their "classic rock" on a headlining tour. So, these guys were motivated to not just show up but also to put on a kickass concert. And with that motivation in hand, they were very receptive to direction, especially Ringo, who was taking a big chance both with me and the band, which featured so many new members. It was his name on the marquee. Yet, by that fifth or sixth song, when someone asked a question, he said, "Just ask Mark. He seems to know everything."

I guess it was his way of saying I'd passed the audition.

27

ABSENT FRIENDS AND MD TO THE STARRS

■ **Brewster, New York, 2021**

I'm looking at an old photograph of the late, great Yogi Horton. It's sitting on my desk. Yogi's got this big smile on his face as he's holding my infant son, Derio, way up in the air. It's a beautiful shot—our first born with a dear friend.

Yogi and I had stayed close after our days playing together at Trax. We all had—Bette, Yogi, Jimi, and me. None of us was too good to forget where we came from. We'd gone through some of the shittiest times together—when there wasn't enough money to pay the rent or the phone bill. But we'd all survived and were now working the biggest stages in the industry. We were all happy.

At least I thought we were.

Not too long after the photo was taken, I was in Japan with Billy when I got a call from Sandra. Yogi, she told me, had committed suicide.

When I got home, I remember asking my father, "Dad, how does this happen?" I mean Yogi was only thirty-three years old.

215

And my father said, "When someone does this, they take their secrets and pain with them. Just try to remember them at their best."

All of these years later, I still try to do that. But it's never easy.

There are more photographs on the desk. Yogi was the first to go, but not the last. There's Carlos Vega . . .

Again, I try to remember how much fun Carlos was on those tours with Simon & Garfunkel. I can still hear his giddy laugh. I don't think of the guy who put a gun to his head.

And it's not always suicide that takes my friends away. Bobby Mayo's photo is on the desk, too. In 2004, Bobby was on tour with Peter Frampton. They'd just played a great show in Basel and Bobby was waiting for the train to take them to the next gig when he suffered a massive heart attack. He was dead before he hit the platform floor.

I gave the eulogy at Bobby's funeral. "Nobody covered more ground or did more on stage than Bobby," I said.

And when T-Bone Wolk died—yes, his photograph is on the desk—I gave his eulogy. Because we were fellow sidemen and I knew the gig. I understood the effort it took and the lack of certainty that came with the job. I understood that no matter the obstacle, we were determined to handle it.

"No problem," is what Bobby always said.

But sometimes it gets to be too much. Sometimes the heart or the soul just gives out.

The Third All Starr Band: (left to right) Felix Cavaliere, Billy Preston, John Entwistle, Ringo Starr, Mark Rivera, Randy Bachman, Mark Farner, Zak Starkey. 1995. (Credit: Henry Diltz)

The Fourth All Starr Band: (top row) Mark Rivera, Simon Kirke, Peter Frampton; (bottom row) Jack Bruce, Ringo Starr, Gary Brooker. 1997. (Credit: Henry Diltz)

I remember one time during my second tour with the All Starrs. The lineup included big shots Peter Frampton, Jack Bruce (Cream), Gary Brooker (Procol Harum), and Simon Kirke (Free, Bad Company). And we're on the plane after a show and Peter Frampton and Jack Bruce are going back and forth, talking about how many records they sold. And you gotta remember, Peter Frampton and Jack Bruce are legends, so they're throwing around some pretty big numbers.

Jack said, "*Disraeli Gears* sold over a million copies."

And Peter said, "Oh, *Frampton Comes Alive* sold *eight* million copies."

And they kept going back and forth, revisiting their catalogs and which album and songs had done what. And while these guys were my heroes—Cream's *Fresh Cream* was one of the records I played the most in 1967—the whole conversation just struck me as absurd. Because not five feet away from these guys and their little pissing contest, was a Beatle with albums like *Sgt. Pepper*, *Abbey Road*, and *Let It Be* still charting!

So I asked Ringo how many albums he sold.

And Ringo shrugged his shoulders and said, "Oh, about a billion."

As you can imagine, the conversation ended there.

■ ■ ■

Let's face it, when it comes to pop music and *Billboard* Top 40, rock 'n' roll is no longer the champion. Not by a long shot. Rap, R&B, dance—these genres have all but erased rock from today's hot charts. And it's no coincidence that right around the time all of that really started, the early '90s, you saw more and more bands like the Who and the Stones getting back together and up on stage. Why? Because fans who love rock 'n' roll weren't getting a ton of new rock music to digest. So what did they do? They turned to their heroes from yesteryear, the greats, who obliged their hunger by once again hitting the road and feeding them a steady stream of rock hits. That's why U2, Bruce, Elton, and Billy all still tour. That's why Kiss and Motley Crüe still tour. Def Leppard, Poison, Metallica . . . any rock band that enjoyed an era of big shows has hungry fans just waiting for the next tour schedule.

But when you tour with a Beatle, you witness that, for the fans, the experience is not merely satisfying a hunger for the music you love. It's not even nostalgia. It's something more, something sacred, like you're taking tea with the queen of England or kneeling before the pope or something. And it doesn't matter where Ringo goes, that reaction is always present.

So, how exactly does Mark Rivera even begin to be a music director for a guy like Ringo? How do you navigate?

In Liverpool, where Ringo grew up, everyone refers to everyone as "you bastard." The word *bastard*, for those guys, can pretty much be used in any situation, good or bad. Like "You're kidding" or "Good one, you bastard." And "You bastard!" which is basically like, "You asshole!" So, it's the tone of how Ringo says it that lets you know what kind of mood he's in. And Ringo's the type of person that if he's in a good mood, he'll give you his Bentley. But if he's in a bad mood, he'll back over you with it. In other words, he's very giving, but don't cross him.

Sometime in 2012, we were just starting rehearsals with the twelfth All Starr Band. This is like my seventh or eighth tour, so I'm firmly established as the music director. And it's a heavy-hitting ensemble. We're talking Steve Lukather (Toto), Gregg Rolie (Santana), Richard Page (Mr. Mister), and Todd Rundgren (Nazz). So, it's probably the first day and Ringo was set to play "Don't Pass Me By" and somebody changed the sound on his keyboard. Probably one of the techs or sound guys: nothing drastic, only the tone of the keyboard. So, he plays the opening chord, but it's the wrong hand positioning. His left hand was supposed to be on octaves on C and his middle finger on a G. But he had it on the Gs with a D in the middle, so it's completely wrong.

And nobody in the band wants to say anything. They're all looking at me, like, "Are you gonna tell Ringo?"

And Ringo goes, "Who fucked with my piano?" He looks right at me and says, "You bastard! You fucking changed everything!" I don't know what the hell he thought I did, that maybe I'd transposed the keys on the keyboard or something. But nothing was wrong with the keyboard. He just hadn't played keys in a while.

Ringo tries it a second time and now gets the right hand wrong. It's gone to shit in a handbag, and he's irate. "Fucking! . . . Fuck you! . . . You bastard!"

So, I walk over to him and I very gently take his hands where they belonged. And then he very calmly plays the chords and we're underway.

The band gets through the whole song without a hitch. And at the end of it, Ringo grabs his microphone and goes, "Mark Rivera!" And because this is in rehearsal, you hear my name bellowing in this empty theater. It's like God is calling down to me.

And I say, "Yeah, Ringo?"

"I'm so sorry."

And you could feel everybody on stage exhale. It was one of those episodes that everyone knows, okay, this could get a bit tricky. I mean, bands have lost members because of lesser moments. It's just the way the business goes. And I remember after that all went down, Steve Lukather looked at me like, "Buddy, you got steel balls."

But, again, Ringo is from Liverpool. He grew up in the ghetto, or what was left of it after the Germans bombed everything. He's tough as nails in terms of attitude and spunk. And for a guy like that who was raised in that "gloves are off" environment and then, suddenly, to be handled the majority of his adult life where the gloves are on, like "we don't want to ruffle his feathers," has to be tough. And he appreciates people who are respectful, but also are able to take the gloves off and treat him the way he is.

And as a kid who grew up navigating personalities in the streets of Brooklyn, I understand how to do that. My upbringing in that neighborhood, in that household with the advice and guidance of my parents, puts me at ease with not only Ringo, who's one of the kindest souls I've ever met, but with any of the other All Starrs. Because sometimes you do have to take the gloves off to get things right.

And it's funny to think how my Ringo gig started with a phone call from George Travis. Again, the universe does amazing things for the sideman who's still on his feet and ready to go. He'd seen me with Billy and Simon & Garfunkel. He knew I wouldn't break under pressure. And he knew that Ringo would need somebody like me, someone who would look after the whole group, and as Ringo says, "put us through our paces." Because the thing about any supergroup is everybody's used to being the star and things going their way. To sort those personalities and give some direction, you need to have somebody who doesn't have a dog in the race. Somebody who's going to look out for the band's interest, not his own—like, "Let's make sure my songs sound great and yours don't sound as good, so I look better." Because that kind of stuff does happen. It's human nature to want your stuff to stand out. So, again, George thought Ringo needed someone who could play all the notes on any instrument required in any style or genre to fit the band's needs, but just as importantly, didn't have a vested interest in one front man over another. And I think George recognized that I had that ability, even before I did, to make it all work. To suggest or correct and not have it misunderstood as ego.

28

HOW IT GOES

Brewster, New York, 2021

Ringo called me up today. Things are starting to open back up and there are some dates on the calendar that might actually happen, including a show with Billy at Madison Square Garden in November. Ringo knows all of this but that's not why he's calling.

Ringo is better known by his friends as "Richie." Over the years and the eleven tours that I've been a member of his band or the musical director, Richie and I have become friends.

"Are you doing okay?" he asks me. My two sons have had some disagreements and they're not speaking to each other right now. This virus and the politics and the physical separation surrounding it have done enough to pull a lot of families apart. Sandra and I pray ours won't be one of them. We think our boys will figure it out, but it's tough.

So, he's calling to cheer me up. We talk for about ten minutes and Ringo tells me things as only a friend could. Telling me, "It's going to be okay, brother. We've all been through it." It says something about the man and what he truly believes. Sideman, front man, superstar, Beatle . . . We're all the same.

Back in 2006, I had to tell Ringo that I couldn't go out on tour with the All Starrs.

And he immediately said, "Are you alright?" In other words, fuck music, are you good?

I said, "I'm fine, Richie. But I have a scheduling problem. Billy's putting a tour together. And I can't afford to say no."

"Oh, you and that piano player," he chuckled. "I guess you love him more than me." And there was this little pause and then he said, "But you'll still be my musical director, right?"

And I remember thinking, *there is a God!* Because no one who ever told Ringo they couldn't do the tour has been asked back. But it was more than that. We'd become good friends and I didn't want that closeness to go away.

In 2010, Joe Walsh got in touch and said, "Hey Mark, July seventh is Ringo's seventieth birthday."

"Yes, I know, Joe," I said. "The All Starrs have a gig at Radio City." I was still the MD but now wasn't usually touring with the group because of my commitment to Billy.

And Joe goes, "Well, Paul wants to do a surprise for Ringo," referring, of course, to Paul McCartney. "Do you know Paul?"

I said, "Yeah, Joe. I know Paul."

And he said, "Great. He wants to sing the song 'Birthday.' Could you put a band together?"

"Absolutely," I said. We got Rick Derringer to join Joe on guitars, Edgar Winter to play keys, Gregg Bissonette on drums, myself, and Paul McCartney on bass. Not too shabby. The plan was we'd come out and do the number as the final encore. *Piece of cake!*

So, Ringo's birthday comes around and we're running a rehearsal a couple hours before the All Starr Band's rehearsal because, again, it's a surprise for Ringo. Now, it's around three o'clock in the afternoon, and one thing about Radio City Music

With my good friend Richie—a.k.a. Ringo Starr—at the Beacon Theatre, NYC, in 2014. (Credit: Scott Ritchie)

Hall is they do tours during the day. So, we're up on stage playing and you could see people walking through the hall looking at us and gasping, like, *I don't fucking believe it. That's Paul McCartney.* And Paul actually waved a few times with this cheeky grin on his face like *Yeah, it's me.* I mean, imagine being those folks, taking a tour of Radio City Music Hall, and, *Oh, by the way, Paul McCartney will be performing as part of the tour.*

Anyway, we're rehearsing "Birthday," which Paul said he hadn't done for about six years. So, we play the song the first time through and Paul says to the rest of us, "How was that?"

And I said, "It was okay, Paul, but you didn't play the bass line straight through."

And everybody in the band sort of froze and started looking at me like, *Oh, this fucking guy's gone. There's no way Paul's gonna put up with this shit.* Because an MD correcting someone like Felix Cavaliere or even Jack Bruce is one thing, but *Paul McCartney?!*

Paul just sort of looked at me and said, "What do you mean?"

And I said, "Well, the bass part goes *doo bop doo bop doooo ohhh.*"

In other words, Paul's bass part plays straight through the song. It doesn't stop like the guitar does.

Paul said, "Right, right, I play straight through."

And everybody breathed a sigh of relief, like, *Okay, so Paul didn't fire him or all of us yet.*

So, we do the song a second time and Paul says to me, "How was *that?*"

And I said, "Well, that was good, except your vocal came in two measures early on '*Yes, we're going to a party, party.*'"

And now everybody's looking at me like not only am I dead meat but I'm also an asshole, like, *Give the guy a fucking break. He just flew in from London to do ONE song . . .*

But I'm saying to myself, *No, we want to do it right. You're the MD and this is how the song goes.*

So with that, Paul says, "I'll tell you what, mate. We'll do it once more time. And this time, I'll play bass, and you sing it. And I'll sort it out."

And I'm like, *Wait? Really!*

So that's what we did. We played the song one more time with me handling the vocals and Paul playing bass. Of course it was totally surreal for me, and while the other band members may have been thinking, *Oh, Mark is so fucked,* I was having a blast. I mean who gets the chance to sing a full-throttle Beatles song with Paul handling the bass and giving you the reins on vocals? It was awesome!

More importantly, it worked. Because when the show came around and it was time for the big encore, Paul was flawless. He came out on stage like a prizefighter and the crowd was going nuts, and he could see how excited Ringo was, and Paul hit the song square in the mouth. He nailed it with a great performance and incredible enthusiasm, coming in at all the right times, hitting all the right notes. And it's funny because if you see the video of that night's performance (like everything else, it's on YouTube) you see Paul look over at me just as we're getting to the *Yes, we're going to a party, party,* acknowledging *Yeah, I'm coming in now.* And that told me that he appreciated the tune-up. Because it had been a while since he'd played the song, and I like to think that me holding his feet to the fire during rehearsals made him that much more confident coming out and playing the tune. And, again, he absolutely crushed it.

And I remember both Joe and Gregg Bissonette coming up to me, smiling, and shaking their heads and saying, "That took balls, man," and "Only you could do that and say that to Paul and get away with it."

But you know what? If somebody hires me as the musical director, it's the same way if kids come over to my house to spend the night—they get treated like my own kids, good or bad. You like it or don't like it? I don't give a shit. This is what I get paid for! And the reason the performance sounds right is because I do have the balls to correct people. It's like "The Emperor's New Clothes." Sometimes you have to be the little kid to say, *You know, Mr. Emperor, you have no knickers on.* That's just the way it is.

Because even the great ones need someone to tell them how it is from time to time.

But obviously, there's no higher rock royalty than Paul. I remember after the show, everyone went back to a party. I mean, it was crazy who was back there that night. *Oh, there's Keith Richards . . . Oh, there's Brian Johnson.* And there's Paul, sitting at a high top with Heather Mills, his wife at the time. And Sandra was with me and I could see her looking over at him. So, we made a left-hand turn, and walked over to Paul and I said, "Excuse me, Paul. I'd like to introduce you to my wife, Sandra."

And Paul stood up and gave her a kiss on the cheek. Or each cheek, if I remember right. And Sandra, who's never starstruck and might not even have been the biggest Beatles fan, was grinning ear to ear. And when we were walking away, I remember joking to her, "You're probably not going to wash your face for a week now, right?"

Because she was like a little girl. Paul kissed her and she was like, *gasp!*

After all, he's a Beatle.

Right: Soundcheck at Radio City Music Hall for Ringo's 70th birthday. July 7, 2010. (Credit: Rob Shanahan)

Left: Discussing "Birthday" with the band. As the musical director, it's my job to make sure we're all on the same page. (Credit: Rob Shanahan) *Below:* (Left to right) Edgar Winter, Mark Rivera, Paul McCartney, Greg Bissonette, Joe Walsh, Rick Derringer. (Credit: Rob Shanahan)

29

HONK THREE TIMES

Brewster, New York, 2020

I head out of the driveway and honk three times. I won't be home until after tomorrow night's gig at the Garden. It seems weird to even think that, much less say it. A gig at the Garden. But it's Beep, Beep, Beep and, somehow, here we are.

We've been through so much. I won't thank the pandemic, but I'll take the time it gave me and Sandra together. The gardening, the long walks, the ping-pong . . .

People think it's pretty far out that we've been together all of these years. It's like the world doesn't believe that rock 'n' roll and a strong marriage compute. Nine times out of ten I'd say the world was right.

Fortunately, Sandra could give two shits about the entertainment business. Otherwise, we would not have lasted. No way. That's been the downfall of so many marriages. Some musician is married to another musician or an actress or a model, and it just never works. I mean "'til death do us part" is hard enough without your spouse saying stuff like, "Hey, honey, can I meet so-and-so? It would be really good for my career." No, thanks. It becomes this game of competing interests.

But what about her? Why did she stay with me all of these years? That's the big question.

We went for therapy sessions a few years ago. The kids were now out of the house and I think Sandra just needed me to understand how difficult it had been and that I needed to do a bit better for our "golden years." And she told the therapist, "Every time Mark left to get on a plane, every time . . . I'd break down in tears."

And when she said that, I started crying. She'd never told me that before, and only then did I realize the full extent of how much the sideman's coming and going tortured her.

When I was home enjoying my family, I was blissfully happy, but also worried about money and was sometimes broke. And when I was out on the road making money and supporting my family, I was miserable. Not miserable playing the shows—just miserable that I had to be away to do it. I was the loneliest guy having a blast in front of twenty thousand people every night, if that makes any sense.

But what can you do? Are you gonna sit around and cry that you don't have your family? Or are you gonna have a great show? And after a great show, are you gonna have a good time or just sit in the hotel room by yourself? It would be 12:30, one o'clock in the morning. I couldn't call Sandra and wake up the house.

So what did you do? You drank and someone had a joint or whatever, and you're back in road mode.

I remember sometime early on with Billy, we did a gig opening up for Tom Jones. And at the end of the night, somebody goes, "Oh, come back to my suite. Tom Jones is gonna join us. And there's a piano there, blah, blah, blah."

So we're all in the room, drunk and high, and Tom Jones finally walks in about two-thirty in the morning with a bottle of cognac and a big cigar. And we start singing Tom Jones songs. And Billy's guitarist, Tommy Byrnes, who's also incredibly talented on keys, started playing the piano. None of us knew the songs, but Tommy's ear would follow along. And I remember Tom Jones saying, "Oh, that's the wrong chord. But I like it." And then he'd take another swig from the bottle. That went on until six in the morning. And Jones, who'd never missed a show in his life, had to cancel the following evening because we'd gone at it so hard. I mean that sort of shit was always happening out on tour. You just got after it.

And being married doesn't mean the carousing stops. It's like Tommy Byrnes, whose wit is as sharp as his ear, would always say, "We're all good men, but there's this little boy inside each of us that wants to come out to play." But the problem is the next morning you're facing the man in the mirror and you think, "I'm such an asshole." Because you know, half a world away or wherever, the rest of your family is together. And whatever they're doing, you missed. You're not a part of it and they're not a part of what you're doing.

Then the tour's over and you're home. You're with the family and everything is great and you think, *When I go out on the road, I'm gonna do better. I'm gonna drink less. I'm gonna carouse less. I'm gonna call more and check in.*

But then you're packing up the gear and it all starts again. Because it's impossible.

I mean, let's say you get to go to Japan or Australia, someplace far away. And initially, it's like, *Hey, man, I'm getting on a first-class flight.* New York, Los Angeles, and then the great beyond. And you're like, *Yeah, man, I got a great gig.* It's like a boys' club and you're hanging with some of your favorite guys in the whole world.

And then you land and your whole body is upside down. And maybe you get a quick phone call home from the hotel room. And it's probably not what you want to hear. The kids are not listening to their mother or someone's got a runny nose. And it's like, well, *what do you want me to do about it? I'm in Japan for the next ten days* . . . Again, you're no longer a part of what they're doing.

And it's not like Sandra's doing this deliberately by any stretch. She's just trying to hold down the fort. But you lose your cool because you can't be honest enough to be angry at yourself for a lack of patience and understanding. So, you go down to the hotel bar and you drink, and you get stupid. And then you're back in front of the mirror the next morning.

Even when the call is about something exciting, you feel disconnected. I remember when Derio was about nine months old and I was off somewhere in Europe. I was in the production office after soundcheck and I was able to make a five-minute phone call. And I called home and Sandra picked up and she was all excited.

"He walked! He walked!" she exclaimed.

Derio had taken his first steps.

And Sandra's brother was there at the house with her, visiting from Switzerland. And Sandra had the phone on speaker.

"You think he could have been here for his steps!" her brother said, laughing. And I could tell he was attempting to lighten the moment because he had to know it was killing both me and Sandra.

And I joked back, "Yeah, fuck you."

But then you're sitting there in this production office that's on the other side of the globe and you hang up the phone and wonder if it's worth it. Because you can't be in two places at once. Not even emotionally.

And then you come home again and they have pictures. Photographs of the boys doing things while you were gone. Birthday parties, events at school. And every time you come home you see the proof. And you think, *see what you missed.*

■ ■ ■

Even early on, as I was scoring amazing gigs, Sandra knew how to keep me grounded. For instance, I was almost in Mick Jagger's solo band. It was after the gig with Yoko, so 1986, and Phil Ashley (Kiss, Tears for Fears) called and said, "I'm doing a project. Mick Jagger is possibly gonna do a solo tour."

And I'm like, "I want in."

Mick auditioned a bunch of sax players, which makes sense. I mean, shit, it's Mick Jagger . . . Anyway, if I remember right, the guy who was just leaving the audition room as I was about to walk in was a guy named Cornelius Bumpus, who played with the Doobie Brothers and Ambrosia. A wonderful, wonderful player and top sax man. Fortunately, Phil told Mick that I could sing as well as play percussion and some second keyboards.

So, I walk in and I remember meeting Doug Wimbish (Living Colour, Sugar Hill Gang). Doug is an amazing bass player. He had these octave dividers and the sound was crazy. Very aggressive player. And then I see Mick, who I hadn't seen since my days at the Record Plant, and it's like *holy shit,* but of course I'm like, "Yeah, it's great to see you, Mick."

Then I met Jeff Beck, who was slated to be the band's guitarist, and I'm just trying to keep my excitement contained. Because this is like *holy fuck.* Jeff Beck was one of my idols. He and Hendrix were my two main guys. And I remember at some point during the rehearsal, I'm looking at Jeff Beck's Marshall—he had a half-stack Marshall. And I had a sax mic. And I stood right in front of Beck's stack because I wanted to feel everything. Just the power of it. And Beck played some line, and I played the same line back to him on the saxophone. And he looked at me like, *Well, that was cool.*

The band played a couple of songs and then Mick decided to do "Gimme Shelter." And as we're playing it, I sang the high Merry Clayton part. *It's just a shot away! It's just a shot away . . .* I went for it and sang it like a maniac. And Mick did like a Mick move, putting his hands on his hips, and went "*WOOH!*" He was like, "Who's that?" And I knew I had the gig.

Later on, during a rehearsal break, we were all just hanging out, and I had to pinch myself because Mick Jagger's to my right, and he passed me a joint. I'm like, *Wow. Mick Jagger just gave me a joint.* So I'm smoking with Mick, and then I turn to my left and it's Jeff Beck. And now I'm passing the joint to Jeff Beck, and it's like, *Where the fuck am I right now?* And I remember his nails were long because he played with his fingers rather than a pick, and they're full of grease because he's a car junkie—he liked those hot rods. And we're just sharing Mick's joint.

I got home that night feeling fucking amazing, like I'd just had the most rock 'n' roll experience of my life, and I said to Sandra, "I'm gonna be in the band and I need to buy some new leather pants." Or something stupid like that. But I was serious. I wanted to be as cool as those fucking guys.

And Sandra said something like, "Okay. If that's what you think."

She'd been with me long enough to know that no deal was a done deal until I was actually up on stage with the act. But Sandra never pulled out the rug from under my enthusiasm. She had her opinion, but it wasn't like, "You're wrong." She would say with humility, "If that's what you think. If that's how you perceive this right now, then okay."

But she wasn't over the moon and jumping for joy, and I felt like saying, *Did you hear me, Sandra? I'm gonna be in a band with Mick Jagger and Jeff Beck.* But Sandra doesn't get all bent out of shape for rock stars the way I do. It's not her passion. And again, it wasn't a done deal. Still, I was pissed and probably went outside to smoke a joint to cool off.

But here's the thing: the gig never happened. Because Jeff Beck and Jagger had a falling out like two or three days later. Why? Who knows. Probably just two alphas locking horns. The whole tour was canceled.

Fast-forward later into the 1980s. I was in my basement music studio, and Sandra came running downstairs with the phone in her hand. I hadn't heard it ring. And she hands me the phone and says, "It's Mick Jagger."

And I'm thinking, *holy fuck,* but I coolly say into the phone "Oh, hi, Mick."

And that iconic, British voice on the other end goes, "Oh, yeah. I decided you should be the sax player in the Rolling Stones."

And I was like, "No shit?!"

So, I got off the phone and for the next two days I was strutting around the house, thinking I'm a badass, again saying stupid shit like, "Yo, I'm gonna be in the Stones. I guess I'd better get some new leather pants!"

And again, Sandra was back with her standard line, "If that's what you think."

What's with this woman?! I'm sure I threw another little hissy fit at her lack of excitement and went back outside to smoke another J.

And sure enough, two days later, I got a call that the Stones gig wasn't gonna happen. Turns out Keith Richards wanted another sax player, Bobby Keys, to be the sax man instead. So Mick apologized, or at least he had his manager call me and apologize for the sudden turnaround. The manager explained that Keith Richards and Bobby Keys were born on the same day and, to Richards, that was a very big deal. Like the same birthdays made him and Bobby Keys kindred souls or some cosmic shit. So, he demanded Keys be the sax player. And that was that. I was in the Rolling Stones for about forty-eight hours.

And once again I had to tell Sandra that I lost the gig. But do you think Sandra crucified me? Do you think she said, "I told you so!"

Absolutely not. Anytime I lost a gig—with Mick Jagger or anyone else—Sandra would just say, "Okay. You'll get the next one." (She'd get more upset when I went outside to smoke a joint than she would over whether or not the gig came through.)

That's incredible fortitude. I mean, I know I'll never be that strong and steady. Every time something goes south, my excitement turns immediately into misery. I go from, "Hooray, all is won!" to "Fuck me, all is lost!" Thank God Sandra doesn't get that way. Sure, I get pissed when I feel like some enthusiasm is in order. But enthusiasm is not what I need. I need steady. I need consistency. Like when I counted steps as a kid, I need to know that something in life will always be dependable and stay the same way and keep the universe from spinning. And as a sideman, where there is no such thing as the dependable gig, Sandra's consistent strength is everything. It keeps our marriage together. It keeps me together. It reminds me, no matter how many times I get down about this business, that I have a family. That I'm a husband. I'm a father. That's what matters.

I remember when the boys were in high school and after their soccer games, we'd have these big dinners at our house afterward. We'd load up the boys and their buddies into the Chevy Blazer and shitty Geo Prizm and come back to the house. And Sandra would cook maybe a big pasta meal or chicken cutlets and potatoes, and there'd be a big salad and bread. She'd spread out as much food as possible and no matter how the game went—win, lose, or draw—the boys were like, "Yeah, we did our best." And they'd have these big smiles. I mean that's the stuff that keeps me sane when I'm out on the road. Just that image, right there.

Because my family is my band. No matter what happens, we will stay together. That's not true for rock bands, especially for the sideman. Again, the rug can be pulled out at any time.

I remember when Billy decided to schedule the River of Dreams tour, I had to tell Daryl Hall and John Oates that I was no longer available. It was 1993.

I'd been working with Daryl and John for more than a year. And I'd been able to really sink my teeth into what Daryl was doing in the studio. Plus, I'd been working close to home so it meant I could be home with Sandra and the boys more often.

So, I told John that I was going back to Billy and he said, "Hey, man. I understand. You gotta do what you gotta do. You're just a sideman."

It wasn't malicious, but when he said that, I remember feeling like shit. Because we'd been at it every day. Working together. And it sort of hit me. *You're just a sideman.* And no matter what he does in this industry, the sideman is always replaceable. John and Daryl would find somebody else. No big deal.

Of course, I knew that already. The sideman's lack of security. But that didn't take the sting away. It was like, *okay, I guess I'll just go now.*

But family is different. Family stays with you. And I owe all of that to Sandra. She lets me come back to something worthwhile. Her arms, our boys. Our home.

Back to the Garden

■ **Madison Square Garden, May 18, 1969**

How I scored the ticket was nothing short of a miracle.

I'd been hanging at the park between Utrecht and Tenth with my big sister Monica. It was only four blocks from our house but may as well have been like going to Sodom and Gomorrah. I loved it. Everything went down at that park: sex, drugs, car racing, people fighting . . . And each neighborhood had their own girls, so every now and then a whole group of dudes from some other park would come over to ours and the place would rumble.

Anyway, I was sixteen years old and I don't know what we were doing there that particular occasion, but it's reasonable to think I was trying to score some pot. Anyway, this neighborhood guy Junio was down there, too, and he had it bad for Monica. He was holding two great tickets to see Jimi Hendrix at MSG that night and asked Monica to go with him. But Monica didn't like the guy. She told him she wanted nothing to do with him.

Junio was so pissed off, and he yelled right at Monica, "Oh, yeah? Well, fuck you!" And he ripped up the tickets and threw them to the ground.

Monica stormed off one way, and Junio in the other. All the people who'd been paying attention put their heads down and turned, not wanting to catch Junio's eye. But not me. All I saw were tickets to Hendrix on the ground.

241

I went over to the scraps and gathered them up. Then, I ran all four blocks home. When I got there, I found some tape and tried to put them back together as best I could. This was long before scanning tickets and all that. I thought, as long as one of these looks any good, I might have a shot. And even though I was just a kid, there was no way I was going to miss a chance at seeing my favorite musician live in concert.

I got one of the tickets to look all right, grabbed some cash, a couple joints, and I was out the door. I hopped the West End train into Madison Square Garden at Thirty-Fourth Street. Usually if I saw a show, it would've been at the Fillmore because MSG had been recently rebuilt and there weren't many shows I would've wanted to see up to that point.

I knew I had to hustle, but I lit up a joint anyway. I wanted to get that buzz going before I went in. And my heart was pounding, thinking, *I hope they let me in with this ticket. I hope they let me in.*

So, I get to the Garden and I'm scanning all the ticket attendants, looking for the right one, the one who'd be cool. I'm just hoping no one's gonna say, "Well, this ticket is invalid, young man."

I chose the youngest-looking guy, and I walked up to him as nonchalant as I could. He looked at me, and I handed him the ticket. He gave it a look, but he didn't say anything about it because I beat him to the punch and said, "Don't even ask."

I have no clue where that line even came from—I'm sure the rock gods were intervening—because the guy took it, tore it so he could get his part of the stub that he needed, and gave me mine. I just stared at the taped up half-a-stub in my hand and looked back up at the young ticket attendant. He nodded, and I walked right past him, stuffing that ticket so far deep in my pocket to keep it safe because my heart was racing, and I wanted to keep that thing for the rest of my life.

Tucked in drawer beside our bed, I've still got the Hendrix ticket! Brewster, NY, 2022. (Credit: Rivera Family Collection)

Inside the venue, it was already popping off. Smoke filled the air, girls were wearing their loose summer dresses, and the first band was taking the stage. It was the Buddy Miles Express, a band I really liked. They were a nine-piece outfit with horns. In fact, I think I was already playing a couple of tunes off this album like "Train" and "Walking down the Highway." So, I was totally into this band.

But when Hendrix came out, it was mind-boggling. His stage was on a slowly rotating turntable, and I'm basically sitting at center ice. So, every time the stage would turn toward me, I would be directly in front of Hendrix's amp—not the PA system, which was pretty good, but his actual guitar amp. It was like that famous Maxell commercial where the guy is sitting in front of a speaker and he gets blown away. Every time Hendrix turned toward me, it was like WHOOSHH! It was insane.

And what had happened back then was that Hendrix would have a lot of trouble with his gear 'cause he pushed everything to the max and then some. And at one point, his guitar and amp crapped out. And I don't remember what song it was that they were doing, but when his gear went down, he pointed to his drummer Mitch Mitchell, who started taking a drum solo. And I swear I can remember this like it was yesterday, Hendrix's amps finally started to come back in. You could hear the *wooh WOOH wooh WOOH*. And he looked over at his band, and they stopped cold.

Then, he broke right into "Spanish Castle Magic."[1] And I noticed immediately that something was different. He was playing it with his right hand, as if he was absolutely right-handed. Then all of a sudden, there was this "yah-dah-daaah" and the stage keeps turning to where Hendrix is right in front of me. That's the moment when the guy, in the middle of playing an incredible lick, threw the guitar around his back and then grabbed it with his other hand and started playing left-handed like he normally does. The crowd goes absolutely mad, and Hendrix continues on with the lick like it was a normal everyday thing.

And I was like, "Holy fuck! Jimi Hendrix just flung the guitar around his back." I was blown away by this guy's showmanship. It was unparalleled. There was nothing I had ever seen like that. I mean, I've even seen Pete Townshend blow up his amplifier, but there's never been anyone meet the bar that Hendrix set. To watch a guy pull a guitar around his back like he was eating a piece of cake. It was unbelievable.

■ ■ ■

1. One of my all-time favorite songs to cover, which I did on my latest album, *Common Bond*. Hendrix got the song's idea from a roadhouse just outside of Seattle called the Spanish Castle, a gig he frequently played in high school.

BACK TO THE GARDEN

■ Madison Square Garden, March 5, 2021

We go on in one hour. It's finally here. A chance to be in the moment. It's what a musician hopes for when he goes up on stage. To leave the rest of the world behind and be one hundred percent present up under the lights. It's his job. It's what the audience has come to experience: a band of musicians giving themselves completely to the music.

And the thing is you never quite know how it's gonna go. Are you gonna bomb? Or, like Hendrix that night in 1969, are you gonna *be* the bomb? (It's like a stand-up comic: tell a joke, people don't laugh, you're not good, you're out of sync. Tell a joke, people laugh and respond, you're good, you're in the pocket.) But good, bad, ugly—I'll take it. Because it's a hell of a lot better than the alternative. And after twenty-one months of no shows, I can honestly say, "I need this."

It's funny, but I've been thinking a lot about Billy's famous lyric: "'Cause he knows that it's me they've been coming to see / To forget about life for a while." It's a line I've heard probably ten thousand times by now, yet it feels so fresh. *Profound*, I guess, is the right word. The whole pandemic, this one feeling has been swimming around in the ether. *When are we gonna get back to the Garden? When are we gonna get back to the stage? To the crowd and their Piano Man?* Because it's not just the audience that needs its medicine. It's all of us. Sideman included. I've needed this for so long now. A chance to keep up with the music and not worry about the previous measures. Because you can't. Not now. Not this show. What's in the past is in the past. What's in the future will make its way. Only the moment matters.

When I tried out for this job, thirty-nine years ago, Billy told me that as long as I wanted a gig in his band, I got it. And in that time, I've never missed a tour. But I almost did.

Again, it was a phone call. 2006. This time it was Max Loubiere, Billy's tour manager, calling to tell me that Billy was heading back out on the road but that I wasn't going to be in the band. And it crushed me. It was the dead of winter and after I got off the phone with Max, I was outside hauling wood for our wood-burning stove, and, while I was trudging through the wet snow, my hand slipped, and the wheelbarrow dumped over.

And I remember picking up the now soaked wood and thinking I was inept. *You can't even keep your family warm.* (And of course, when I came inside and told Sandra what had happened, she was the strong one, telling me we would get past this.)

But where had I gone wrong?

It didn't take long for me to realize that my appreciation for the opportunity to be Billy Joel's sax player had grown a bit lax. And maybe I'd gotten a little too demanding. Like, "Hey, I deserve this or that . . ." and I'd adopted a sense of entitlement. It happens. Sidemen think they should start being treated like the stars, which is total bullshit. *You're getting paid, you're doing a job. You're entitled to what's being given to you. Nothing else.*

And for the performer, a lack of appreciation for the gig is death. Because the secret to being able to live in the moment, is appreciating the moment. Being grateful for its existence. For the opportunity. *Hey, I get this amazing chance to play with one of the greatest songwriters and bands in history. I'm one of the luckiest sonuvabitches in the world!*

And the more gratitude you have for the moment, the more you can be absorbed in it.

That's the way I felt when I first hit the road with Sam & Dave. That twenty-year-old kid who was delighted to be up on a big stage had never gone away. Except now, after Billy essentially fired me, I understood that maybe that kid *had* gone away, and I needed to bring him back.

I always say that performance is like oxygen. I need it to survive. Well, starve a man of his oxygen and he'll better appreciate the air he breathes. And it was a tough lesson to learn because I'd been Billy Joel's sax player for so long. It was my identity. And to lose it felt like I was starting over again. I was back in the city doing shitty club dates, working the hustle as hard as I'd done it forty years earlier. And I sent a letter off to Billy, thanking him for all of the opportunities he'd given me, not to win him back but to basically say what I'd failed to say for a while. "Thank you."

Fortunately, a few months later, the phone rang again. Billy wanted me back in the band and I was up on my riser for the first show. So, the streak continued and now we're going on forty years . . .

Here we are again. Back in the band after a long stretch of no shows. Of oxygen deprivation. And how many times have we been praying for it? This chance to breathe? And the truth is none of us knows how long this will last. Maybe tomorrow the pandemic will come back. Like John Lennon said, "Tomorrow Never Knows."

So, really, all we have is this moment. And it means the world to me. To pull all of that air into my lungs and then blow it out into a saxophone for the crowd to hear. I'm so grateful for it. Nothing else matters.

Yeah, I'm feeling pretty good. It's gonna be a great show.

Back on stage with Billy at Madison Square
Garden, 2022. (Credit: Myrna Suárez)

ACKNOWLEDGMENTS

bove all, I thank my father, Deider Rivera. The most loving and grateful man I've ever known. He was taken much too soon but he's with me ALL-WAYS . . . My mom, Angela Stella Crocco Rivera, whose kindness knew no limits. I held her hand as she took her last breath. She would always say, "No good can come from bad words."

My foundation, my rock, my bride, Sandra. She never stopped believing in us and gave me our most precious gifts of all, our sons Derio and Moreo. Melissa and our hope for the future, our grandson Vedder Neruda Rivera.

My sisters, Monica and Gloria, for putting up with me ALL those years . . . And to my Uncle Vinny, my godfather and the man who gave me my first saxophone lesson.

A very special thanks to Finn and Kim Wentworth. Without them these words would never have been heard.

My lifelong friend John Grado (Jr. Beatle) and his family. Alan Phillips, who never gave up on my dreams. Jeff Ader and his amazing record collection. Paul Stawinski, who saw some of the darkest times and provided love. Jimmy Bralower, who constantly reminded me, "Buddy, THIS is how it goes." Kenny Papa, Rick "Spunky" Pascual, Jon Cobert, Daryl Leoce, Ted Leonsis. To my doctor, Thomas Burnette ("Yo, Dr. T!"), and his amazing family for their love, friendship, and guidance over the years. Lisa Gunn, who along with Joel Himelfarb got Sandra and me through our bout with COVID in March 2020, Dorothy, Rocky, and Sophie Tancredi. They will always a have a loving place in my heart. The entire Yamaha family, especially John Wittman, Chris Gero, and Tamogi Hirakata. To my good friends Myrna Suárez and Brian and Linda Mantai for their constant willingness to go the extra mile—I thank you!

Billy Joel's touring band and crew—the GREATEST group I've ever known! Starting with Brian Ruggles, Steve Cohen, Michael Grizel, the Thrashers, Wayne Williams, Rick "Chainsaw" LePointe, Mark Snyder, Liz Mahon, Merissa Czajkowski, Josh Weibel, "Jay" Yochem, Joe Weir, Mark Foffano, Simon Cadiz, Zainool Hamid, Vinny Palafrone, Sean Fox, Jerry Fox, Larry Dolby, Noel Rush, Bob Bender, Tim Brockman, Mike Colucci, and Claire Mercuri. Together they are the lightning rod that protects us. PLEASE forgive me as I can't list you all.

Oh, yes—and the band! Tommy Byrnes, Crystal Taliefero, David Rosenthal, Chuck Burgi, Andy Cichon, Carl Fischer, and Michael Delgudice.

Dennis Arfa ("We Won't Fuck It Up"), Max Loubiere, Todd Kamelhard, Bruce Grakal, George Travis, Dave Hart, Scotty "My Son, My Son" Ritchie, Jeff Chonis, and two of the finest musicians I've ever performed with, Gregg Bissonette and Steve "Luke" Lukather.

A special thank you to Mike Poncy and his family for sacrificing so much of their time to allow this book to come together.

And to each and every musician that I have been blessed to share a stage with. I am the product of all our time together.

To Billy Joel, for keeping his promise and allowing me this amazing journey. Hopefully, I'm fulfilling my part of our bargain.

ACKNOWLEDGMENTS

To Ringo Starr. You, my friend, reminded me what a gift simply playing our music IS, and you always exemplify peace, love, and gratitude.

And finally, Robert John "Mutt" Lange. He always brought "the vibe" and was the first to believe that I had a voice and helped me to believe that this voice must be heard . . .

With much love, gratitude, and hope always . . . MR अहिं सा

MARK RIVERA'S BAND AND PERFORMANCE TIMELINE AND HIGHLIGHTS

1967-1973

Population 4: 1967
MR: Bass Guitar, Sax, Vocals

Maitrex Square: 1968 and 1969
MR: Sax, Guitar, Vocals

Pecker Frost: 1969
MR: Sax, Flute, Rhythm Guitar, Keyboards, Vocals

Jam Band: 1969
MR: Sax & Vocals

Tulsa: 1970
MR: Sax, Flute, Percussion, Vocals

Truth: 1970
MR: Sax, Flute, Vocals

Straight Jacket: 1970
MR: Sax, Flute, Percussion, Vocals

Eclipse: 1971
MR: Vocals

Marty Castore Bands: Late 1971
MR: Sax & Vocals

Double F Band: 1972
MR: Sax, Flute, Vocals

Home Brew: 1972
MR: Sax, Flute, Vocals

Our Gang: 1973
MR: Sax, Flute, Vocals

General Meek: 1973
MR: Flute & Vocals

1974-1980

Sam & Dave: 1974
MR: Alto & Bari Sax

Essence: 1974
MR: Sax, Flute, Guitar, Keyboards, Vocals

Latin Band: Early 1974
MR: Bass

Joey Dambra Band: 1974
MR: Sax & Vocals

Dog Soldier/BOMF: 1975-78
MR: Sax, Flute, Vocals

The Valentino Band: 1978
MR: Sax, Flute, Vocals

Cash/Tycoon: 1978-79
MR: Sax, Vocals

Jimmy Frank & Trouble: 1978-80
MR: Sax, Vocals, Percussion

Numerous Pickup Bands . . . too many to list: 1979-81

TRAX Bands: 1978-81
MR: Sax, Flute, Percussion, Vocals

Blue Oyster Cult *Cultosaurus Erectus*: 1980
MR: Sax

1981-1994

Benny Marrones *Too Much to Lose*: 1981
MR: Sax

Foreigner *4*: 1981
MR: Sax, Vocals

Foreigner 4 tour: 1981-1982
MR: Sax, Flute, Guitar, Keyboards, Vocals

Billy Joel Nylon Curtain tour: 1982
MR: Sax, Flute, Keyboards, Percussion, Vocals

Simon & Garfunkel Summer Evening tour: 1983
MR: Sax

Paul Simon *Hearts and Bones*: 1983
MR: Sax

Billy Joel Innocent Man tour: 1984
MR: Sax, Flute, Keyboards, Percussion, Vocals

Peter Gabriel *So*: 1985
MR: Sax

PERFORMANCE TIMELINE AND HIGHLIGHTS

Billy Ocean *Love Zone*: 1986
MR: Sax

Foreigner *Agent Provocateur* album/tour: 1985-86
MR: Sax, Flute, Guitar, Keyboards, Vocals

Yoko Band: 1986
MR: Sax, Flute, Guitar, Keyboards, Vocals

Peter Hoffman "Elvis" tour: 1986
MR: Sax & Vocals

Billy Joel The Bridge tour: 1986-87
MR: Sax, Flute, Keyboards, Percussion, Vocals

Joe Walsh *Got Any Gum?*: 1987
MR: Sax

Billy Joel *Kohuept* album/tour: 1987
MR: Sax, Flute, Keyboards, Percussion, Vocals

Hall & Oates *Ooh Yeah!* album/tour: 1988
MR: Sax, Flute, Percussion, Keyboards, Vocals

Billy Joel Stormfront tour: 1989-90
MR: Sax, Flute, Keyboards, Percussion, Vocals

Foreigner Unusual Heat tour: 1991
MR: Sax, Flute, Guitar, Keyboards, Vocals

Billy Joel River of Dreams tour: 1991
MR: Sax, Flute, Percussion, Vocals

Billy Joel & Elton John Face to Face tour: 1994 and 1995
MR: Sax, Flute, Keyboards, Vocals

PERFORMANCE TIMELINE AND HIGHLIGHTS

1995-Present

Ringo Starr and His All Starr Band: 1995
Featuring: Ringo Starr, Billy Preston, John Entwistle, Mark Farner, Randy Bachman, Felix Cavaliere, Zak Starkey
MR: Sax, Guitar, Keyboards, Percussion, Vocals (Musical Director)

Ringo Starr and His All Starr Band: 1997-98
Featuring: Ringo Starr, Peter Frampton, Jack Bruce, Gary Brooker, Simon Kirke
MR: Sax Keyboards, Percussion, Vocals (MD)

Ringo Starr and His All Starr Band: 2000
Featuring: Ringo Starr, Jack Bruce, Eric Carmen, Simon Kirke, Dave Edmonds
MR: Sax, Harmonica, Percussion, Vocals (Musical Director)

Ringo Starr and His All Starr Band: 2001
Featuring: Ringo Starr, Greg Lake, Roger Hodgson, Ian Hunter, Howard Jones, Shelia E.
MR: Sax, Flute, Harmonica, Bass, Guitar, Percussion, Vocals (Musical Director)

Billy Joel and Elton John Face to Face tour: 2001, 2002, 2003 (multiple tours)
MR: Sax, Flute, Keyboards, Vocals

Ringo Starr and His All Starr Band: 2003
Featuring: Ringo Starr, Colin Hay, John Waite, Paul Carrack, Sheila E.
MR: Sax, Flute, Bass, Guitar, Harmonica, Percussion, Vocals (Musical Director)

Billy Joel: 2006-2013 (multiple tours and individual performances)
MR: Sax, Flute, Keyboards, Vocals

PERFORMANCE TIMELINE AND HIGHLIGHTS

Ringo Starr and His All Starr Band: 2006-2012 (multiple tours)
MR: Musical Director (did not tour due to Billy Joel commitment)

Dear Mr. Fantasy: A Tribute to Jim Capaldi: 2007
Featuring: Stevie Winwood, Pete Townshend, Joe Walsh, Jon Lord, Paul Weller, Yusuf Islam (a.k.a. Cat Stevens), Gary Moore
MR: Musical Director

Billy Joel *Last Play at Shea*: 2008
Featuring: Sir Paul McCartney, Tony Bennett, Don Henley, Steven Tyler, Roger Daltrey, John Mellencamp, Garth Brooks, John Mayer
MR: Sax, Flute, Keyboards, Vocals

Billy Joel and Elton John Face to Face tour: 2009-2010
MR: Sax, Flute, Keyboards, Vocals

Ringo Starr's 70th Birthday Celebration: 2010
Featuring: Paul McCartney, Joe Walsh, Edgar Winter, Rick Derringer, Gregg Bissonette
MR: Musical Director, Percussion, Vocals

Ringo Starr and His All Starr Band: 2013
Featuring: Ringo Starr, Steve Lukather, Richard Page, Todd Rundgren, Gregg Rolie, Gregg Bissonette
MR: Sax, Keyboards, Percussion, Vocals (Musical Director)

Billy Joel in Concert: 2014-present
MR: Sax, Flute, Keyboards, Vocals

Mark Rivera *Common Bond* (album): 2014

Mark Rivera's '67 Chevy (band); Glad: "The Music of Traffic" (band): 2014-present

ABOUT THE AUTHORS

Credit: Myrna Suárez

MARK RIVERA is best known as Billy Joel's saxophonist, as well as Musical Director for Ringo Starr and His All Starr Band. Rivera is a multi-instrumentalist and vocalist who over the past fifty years has shared the stage and supported some of rock 'n' roll's greatest performers, including John Lennon, Paul McCartney, Elton John, Simon & Garfunkel, Foreigner, Peter Frampton, Tony Bennett, Joe Walsh, Hall & Oates, and Peter Gabriel.

Rivera lives in upstate New York with his wife, Sandra. They have two adult children and one grandchild.

MIKE PONCY is a writer and musician living in central Virginia with his wife, Amanda, and their two children. The last book he co-developed was the *New York Times* bestseller *I'm Keith Hernandez*.